Investment Policy Review

UKRAINE

OECD

ORGANISATION FOR ECONOMIC CO-OPERATION AND DEVELOPMENT

ORGANISATION FOR ECONOMIC CO-OPERATION AND DEVELOPMENT

Pursuant to Article 1 of the Convention signed in Paris on 14th December 1960, and which came into force on 30th September 1961, the Organisation for Economic Co-operation and Development (OECD) shall promote policies designed:

- to achieve the highest sustainable economic growth and employment and a rising standard of living in Member countries, while maintaining financial stability, and thus to contribute to the development of the world economy;
- to contribute to sound economic expansion in Member as well as non-member countries in the process of economic development; and
- to contribute to the expansion of world trade on a multilateral, non-discriminatory basis in accordance with international obligations.

The original Member countries of the OECD are Austria, Belgium, Canada, Denmark, France, Germany, Greece, Iceland, Ireland, Italy, Luxembourg, the Netherlands, Norway, Portugal, Spain, Sweden, Switzerland, Turkey, the United Kingdom and the United States. The following countries became Members subsequently through accession at the dates indicated hereafter: Japan (28th April 1964), Finland (28th January 1969), Australia (7th June 1971), New Zealand (29th May 1973), Mexico (18th May 1994), the Czech Republic (21st December 1995), Hungary (7th May 1996), Poland (22nd November 1996), Korea (12th December 1996) and the Slovak Republic (14h December 2000). The Commission of the European Communities takes part in the work of the OECD (Article 13 of the OECD Convention).

OECD CENTRE FOR CO-OPERATION WITH NON-MEMBERS

The OECD Centre for Co-operation with Non-Members (CCNM) promotes and co-ordinates OECD's policy dialogue and co-operation with economies outside the OECD area. The OECD currently maintains policy co-operation with approximately 70 non-Member economies.

The essence of CCNM co-operative programmes with non-Members is to make the rich and varied assets of the OECD available beyond its current Membership to interested non-Members. For example, the OECD's unique co-operative working methods that have been developed over many years; a stock of best practices across all areas of public policy experiences among Members; on-going policy dialogue among senior representatives from capitals, reinforced by reciprocal peer pressure; and the capacity to address interdisciplinary issues. All of this is supported by a rich historical database and strong analytical capacity within the Secretariat. Likewise, Member countries benefit from the exchange of experience with experts and officials from non-Member economies.

The CCNM's programmes cover the major policy areas of OECD expertise that are of mutual interest to non-Members. These include: economic monitoring, structural adjustment through sectoral policies, trade policy, international investment, financial sector reform, international taxation, environment, agriculture, labour market, education and social policy, as well as innovation and technological policy development

Publié en français sous le titre :
EXAMEN DES POLITIQUES D'INVESTISSEMENT
Ukraine

Foreword

The Investment Policy Review of Ukraine builds on the earlier "Investment Guide for Ukraine", published in 1993 to provide information to business operators planning activities in Ukraine. This Review, which is prepared in the framework of the OECD's Centre for Co-operation with Non-Members, is intended to advance the policy dialogue and co-operation between the OECD and Ukrainian decision-makers on investment issues. To support Ukraine's reform efforts, the Review assesses the implementation of the legal rules, with an emphasis on their practical enforcement, and identifies gaps in legislation and institutional frameworks, distilling an array of policy recommendations.

In addition to the legal and institutional setting specifically dealing with foreign investment issues, the Review encompasses salient features of the overall business environment in Ukraine, such as legislation ensuring the rule of law, contract and property protection, corporate legislation, secured lending and financial sector legislation, taxation, and, public governance, privatisation, competition and anti-corruption measures. It sets out the main impediments to investment and private sector development in Ukraine focusing on government regulations for foreign investment.

Mehmet Ögütçü co-ordinated and finalised the Review under the guidance of Rainer Geiger, with the technical assistance from Jennifer MacGillivray and Edward Smiley. Recommendations have been drafted by Juergen Voss, with the advice of Vladimir Anatoliyevitch Ignatchenko, Anatoly Dovgert and significant inputs from Yaroslav Kinakh. Other major contributors from the OECD Secretariat included Jan Schuijer and Fianna Jesover. The Review also benefited from comments on different chapters by Tristan Price, Eva Thiel, Frederic Wehrle, Terry Winslow, Sebastian Molineus, Elena Miteva and Marie-Laurence Guy of the OECD Secretariat, as well as editing assistance from George Williamson.

Valuable contributions are acknowledged from Victor Ivanovitch Lisitsky, State Secretary of the Cabinet of Ministers of Ukraine, the Ministry of Economy of Ukraine, the Ministry of Foreign Affairs (Oleg Skoropad in particular), the World Bank Group, the Organisation for Security and Co-operation in Europe, the Deloitte Touche Tohmatsu USAID Commercial Law Center Project (Prof. Viktor Musiyaka and Dr. Petro Matiaszek in particular), the International Center for Policy

Studies, the Ukrainian-European Policy and Legal Advice Centre, the Kiev law offices of Baker & McKenzie, Salkom, Frishberg & Partners, Proxen & Partners, Jurvneshservice, and the German Advisory Group on Economic Reforms to the Ukrainian Government. We gratefully acknowledge the support provided by the Government of Poland for investment work on Ukraine including from Marek Wejtko of the Polish Delegation to the OECD.

Several members of the Business and Industry Advisory Committee (BIAC) to the OECD including Denizhan Erocal, Charles Kovacs, Andrey Pleskonos, Elodie Ritzenthaler, Dr. Irina Paliashvili and Ms. Liselott Agerlid took an active part in its preparation. Among many others, David L. Konick, Marek Dabrowski, Philip Davies, Andrey Nikitov, Rudolf Mueller, Scott McLeod, Thomas Vennen and Michel Zayet provided useful inputs to the Review, particularly on recommendations.

Draft of the Review was released and discussed at an OECD-Ukraine Roundtable in Kiev on 23 February 2001. Participants at the meeting called for the establishment of a joint Forum on Investment and Enterprise Development to follow up the implementation of the recommendations proposed in the Review, and develop further actions to help Ukraine improve its investment environment.

This Review, current as of March 2001, is published on the responsibility of the Secretary-General of the OECD.

Eric Burgeat
Director
Centre for Co-operation with Non-Members

Statement from the Government of Ukraine

The Government of Ukraine is especially grateful to the Centre for Co-operation with Non-Members and the Directorate for Fiscal, Financial and Enterprise Affairs of the Organisation for Economic Co-operation and Development (OECD) for their invaluable work in preparing this Policy Review.

Unlike other analyses of the difficulties and shortcomings in Ukraine's investment climate and business conditions, this Investment Policy Review identifies key issues and offers very practical suggestions for modifying and improving our legal and regulatory environment in order to attract further investments and provide for an attractive environment for business. We will introduce measures to implement these policy recommendations.

Our government is well aware of the importance of encouraging the development and growth of the private sector in our economy. We also recognise that foreign direct investment plays a particularly significant role in accelerating the growth and development of our economy. Accordingly, the recommendations herein, together with the broad range of policy reforms we are implementing to restructure our economy, are invaluable and useful tools to guide us during this transition process.

In a broader context, we look forward to more extensive and deeper co-operation with the OECD. The OECD has a unique ability to harness and convey practical and policy experience of its Member countries; Ukraine needs and wants such experience. We therefore look forward to the newly created OECD-Ukraine Forum on Investment and Enterprise Development as our first and formal step in building a closer relationship with the OECD, and learning from the experience of its Member countries.

Victor Lysytsky
State Secretary
of the Cabinet of the Government of Ukraine

Table of contents

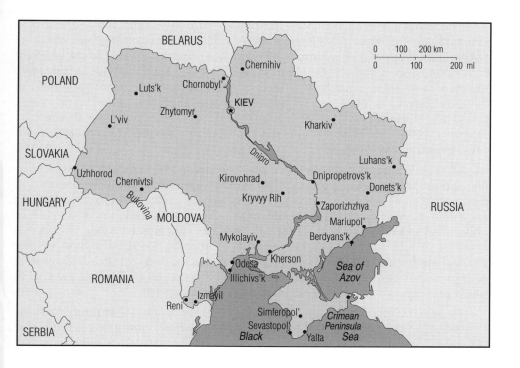

Introduction

The present OECD Review has been carried out at the request of the Government of Ukraine – not as a desktop study, but in a dynamic framework as a joint exercise involving almost all key players, domestic and international alike, on Ukraine's investment scene. It identifies the obstacles to investment and private sector development, and puts forth concrete, practical recommendations for an improved business climate. This version of the Review incorporates comments and suggestions received during and after the Roundtable meeting on 23 February 2001, co-organised by the OECD and Ukraine, with the support of the Deloitte Touche Tohmatsu USAID Commercial Law Center Project based in Kiev.

The concluding statement of the Kiev Roundtable meeting was: *"Ukraine has the potential to be transformed from 'a miracle in waiting' to 'a miracle in making'"* in recognition of this nation's rich human and natural resource endowment, as well as strategic location. Senior government officials supported the Review's recommendations and pledged strong support to implementing them in conformity with the government's strategic objectives for 2001 and beyond.

The most pressing economic problems currently facing Ukraine are of a structural nature: slow privatisation; little industrial restructuring; an unwieldy governmental apparatus; a narrow tax base; over-regulation; significant levels of corruption; and a largely unreformed agricultural sector. These factors have resulted in pushing over half of the economy to operate in the informal, or "shadow", sector. While foreign assistance is crucial in this period of economic transition, official flows of assistance in the longer term could be dwarfed by private capital inflows if Ukraine creates a more conducive environment for private sector development.

Ukraine is a potentially attractive place to invest. The failure to attract foreign investment, the staggering capital flight, the collapse of the formal economy and the relative growth of the "shadow" economy are in sharp contrast to certain strong endowments of Ukraine. The country possesses a large amount of unused or underused physical and human capital (98.6 per cent literacy rate), substantial reserves of idle savings, a large domestic market of about 50 million people (among the largest in Europe), rich natural resources, and a strategic location at the crossroads of Central Europe, Russia, Central Asia and the Middle East, all of which provide a solid base for sustainable economic growth.

Hence, the relative economic decline of Ukraine cannot be attributed merely to economic fundamentals, but is mainly due to difficult conditions for business activity in Ukraine that deter investors, foreign and domestic alike, drive Ukrainian entrepreneurs underground and encourage domestic capital to flee the country. In fact, virtually all international ratings and investment climate surveys place Ukraine among the least advanced transition economies. In particular, Ukraine has lagged behind other Eastern and Central European countries in attracting FDI flows.

From a sector perspective, as of January 2000, the main destination of FDI in Ukraine, was the domestic food industry (20 per cent of cumulative FDI), followed by domestic trade operations (over 17 per cent) and mechanical engineering/metals (almost 11 per cent). By origin of investment, the United States has been the dominant foreign investor. United States companies have made investments valued at some $590 million, representing 18 per cent of all FDI made in Ukraine. The United States is followed by the Netherlands with 9 per cent, the Russian Federation (9 per cent), Germany (7 per cent) and the United Kingdom (7 per cent).

Ukraine's investment needs are huge, as large parts of the capital stock have in fact no longer been maintained or replaced during the last decade, not to speak of enlargement. There is certainly also an important need for renewal of the general infrastructure. Investments needed for rehabilitating the ailing infrastructure alone are estimated to exceed $40 billion. According to official Ukrainian data, as of early January 2001, the cumulative FDI inflows into Ukraine since 1991 approached $3.9 billion.[1] On a per capita basis, foreign direct investment is among the lowest in the region – $79 per capita, placing Ukraine as the second lowest among Commonwealth of Independent States (CIS), ahead of Belarus only, and with less than 10 per cent of the FDI that has flowed to Poland or Hungary. The hostile business environment has contributed to substantial capital outflows, estimated to exceed $10 to $20 billion since independence at a time when Ukraine badly needs resources for domestic investment. President Leonid Kuchma has proposed a new law in September 2000, which would grant amnesty to "shadow" capital, allowing Ukrainians to legalise any hidden assets. They would simply have to declare the account to the tax authorities, transfer it from any foreign bank to a Ukrainian bank, and pay a 10 per cent tax on it.

The transition process in Ukraine has been difficult, burdened as the country is with the economic structure it inherited from its Soviet past, the uncertainties and a complex political constellation. Starting in late 1996, Ukraine's Government initiated a comprehensive legislative programme to remove structural obstacles to economic growth. It included tax reduction, regulatory reform, budget cuts and pension reform. Indeed, bold and extensive economic reforms are vital, not least to ensure the sharp increase in foreign investment, which the country needs. High and seemingly arbitrarily applied taxes have scared investors off. Privatisation – an important vehicle for foreign investment and economic reform in many countries – has been slow and has suffered setbacks, such as in agriculture. Rules prejudicial to foreign investment in privatised industries continue to apply.

Many difficulties stem from a bureaucracy, which is well entrenched and still extensive, and still operates with a mindset reflecting the FSU legacy of control and strict regulation, as well as from complex and often ambiguous legislation. Administrative reforms have been slow, and not sufficiently deep and extensive. And the legislative and regulatory changes have not been oriented towards establishing explicit and transparent rules of the game. This, of course, invites inconsistent interpretation and unpredictable application of laws and regulations, with the added problem of corruption.

Major amendments of Ukraine's FDI legislation have been enacted during the past few years. These changes have been fundamental, since they constituted a shift from a generous, but ineffective system of specific incentives to a system of non-discriminatory legal conditions for all investors, including more extensive investment protection. Ukraine has also signed a significant number of bilateral investment treaties, including those with some OECD Member countries. These legislative steps lend further credence to the notion that incentives, however generous, can be no substitute for those factors that really attract foreign investors: a promising market, transparent and non-discriminatory legislation, effective investment protection and sound economic policies. Given the massive need of foreign investment for industrial restructuring, a rapid improvement of Ukraine's investment climate is indeed urgent.

To maximise Ukraine's potential for foreign investors, it is clear that the government needs to swiftly proceed with more privatisation in a transparent and non-discriminatory fashion, develop a business climate conducive to the rapid expansion of foreign trade, limit tariff and non-tariff barriers, ensure fair access to the Ukrainian market for foreign firms and foster a meaningful dialogue with businesses on key policy issues. The Review, reflecting the expertise and recommendations of the OECD Secretariat, Member countries, other international organisations, the international business community, many Ukrainian officials and business executives, forms a solid basis for further follow-up and monitoring of policy reforms in Ukraine.

The key issue that arose throughout the 23 February discussions remains: who will be charged and empowered to implement these recommendations. Timing was of critical importance: when will the implementation commence and what timelines and identified benchmarks would be to track performance. It was strongly recommended to establish an inter-ministerial/department team to develop a strategy to begin implementing the recommendations and rectifying the shortcomings identified in the Review. This team would also be the interface of the Ukrainian government with the OECD-Ukraine Forum on Investment and Enterprise Development, established during the Roundtable. The Forum will help develop dialogue and synergies among government officials, the private sector, bilateral and multilateral co-operation programmes, and above all, help identify the fundamentals of a forward-looking investment policy (see the Forum's Terms of Reference in Annex 5).

Executive Summary and Recommendations

Overview

Ukraine is the only eastern European transition economy that experienced a decline until last year of its GDP and erosion of living standards in every year since independence in 1991. According to official (though not entirely reliable) statistics, its GDP by 1998 had plummeted to about 37 per cent and real average wages to 31 per cent of pre-independence levels. More than half of the population reportedly lives below the poverty line.

The virtual collapse of the formal economy came hand-in-glove with a steady increase of the shadow economy. The causes of the rapid development of the shadow economy in Ukraine are closely related to the dissolution of the old political and economic systems and, subsequently, to delayed economic reforms. The official estimates of the shadow economy by *Derzhcomstat* claim that its share is roughly 13-14 per cent of official GDP. It should be stressed that this amount is included in official estimates. However, more realistic estimates range between 50 and 70 per cent of official GDP in 2000. While the shadow economy somewhat compensates for the decline of the formal economy, it also increases distortions in the Ukrainian economy, with allegations of corruption pervading all layers of the state.

Business operators in Ukraine still face an omnipresent bureaucracy, over-regulation, corruption, considerable legal uncertainty and stifling tax and customs structures. Fiscal deficits and arrears remain huge, both with respect to the government and among enterprises. As a result, private lending is only available on short term and at exorbitant rates. While most small and medium-sized enterprises have been privatised, more than 200 large enterprises accounting for some 70 per cent of industrial output are still controlled by the state. The parallel operation of state and private enterprises in the Ukrainian market distorts competition. After hyperinflation in 1993, inflation rates now cluster around 20 per cent per annum. Trade tariffs have been liberalised but considerable non-tariff barriers remain.

After almost ten years of independence, reforms to establish a market economy under the rule of law are still in an embryonic state. This is largely due to the paralysis, which existed until the end of 1999 between a reform-oriented President and a Parliament with a reform-sceptical majority. Subsequent to the re-election of President Leonid Kuchma in November 1999, a referendum on amendments to the Constitution strengthening the presidency, and parliamentary by-elections in spring 2000, a new, albeit fragile, majority has been formed in Parliament (*Verkhovna Rada*) in support of market-oriented reforms. For the first time, the political constellation appears to be conducive to adopting reform legislation.

In the first half of 2000, a comprehensive reform programme was launched and first achievements can be seen, notably the adoption of a relatively balanced budget (with a deficit of some 1.5-2.0 per cent of GDP) and the successful renegotiation of Ukraine's external debt. While still incomplete and debatable in detail, the pending reforms do go in the right direction and, if implemented, will considerably enhance the investment climate in Ukraine. Ukraine attracted a record $750 million in foreign direct investment in 2000. In 2000, also for the first time, Ukraine's real GDP growth was 6 per cent. The Government predicts a real GDP growth of at least 4 per cent in 2001.[2] Thus there now appears to be an opportunity for economic reversal. Whether it will materialise or not will depend in large measure on whether the reform process will be carried forward decisively.

Despite the difficulties of moving ahead simultaneously on a myriad of issues, reforms must be pursued as an integrated process, since success depends on the interaction of reform measures in the various areas. Implementation of the necessary reform agenda takes time. To mobilise investments now, it is necessary to market the reform programme and build investor confidence in its decisive implementation, persuading investors that it pays to buy into the Ukrainian economy today (when entry prices are still moderate) and reap returns tomorrow (when business conditions will be favourable).

Foreign Investment Regime

Rules for foreign investments as distinguished from domestic are found in both domestic legislation and international treaties of Ukraine; they govern both the admission of foreign investments (pre-establishment treatment) and their protection once admitted (post-establishment treatment). Some legislation also, while not expressly distinguishing between domestic and foreign investment, in practice applies to foreign investment only, notably the laws on production-sharing and concession agreements. Foreign investments are furthermore subject to particular administrative procedures (registration and dispute settlement). In several cases, legislation applicable in principle to both domestic and foreign investment alike includes provisions that apply to foreign investment only.

Investment Protection

The basic rules on the (post-establishment) treatment of foreign investments are set out in the "Law on the Regime of Foreign Investment" of March 1996. This law has several shortcomings; it is in particular flawed by a total of 27 provisos giving precedence to domestic legislation. In particular, a proviso limits the principle of national treatment. In theory, the Law protects foreign investors against discrimination *vis-à-vis* domestic investors – but only to the extent that no discriminatory provision is found in generally applicable legislation.

The shortcomings of investment protection under domestic legislation are, however, largely remedied by the considerable and still expanding network of international treaties of Ukraine applying to international investments. Ukraine has concluded some 67 bilateral investment protection treaties ("BITs"), 43 of which are in force. In most cases these treaties conform to international standards. In addition, Ukraine has signed several multilateral agreements related to foreign investment, especially the ICSID Convention of 1965 (ratified on 16 March 2000), the 1994 Energy Charter Treaty, and the 1998 Partnership and Co-operation Agreement with the European Union. These treaties are integral parts of the Ukrainian legal system, directly applicable and prevailing over domestic legislation in case of conflict.

While the legal protection can thus be considered as adequate for most foreign investments (*i.e.* investments from countries with which Ukraine has a BIT), it is nevertheless proposed to align the Foreign Investment Law with the protection provided by the treaty framework. More specifically, it is recommended to:

- review the necessity of the frequent provisos in favour of generally applicable Ukrainian legislation and delete these provisos wherever feasible. Especially the proviso with respect to national treatment, which is inconsistent with the treaty framework, should be either deleted or at least replaced by a list of exceptions from this principle, to be attached to the Foreign Investment Law;

- extend the protection of expropriation and nationalisation to indirect and creeping expropriation; and

- upon ratification of the ICSID Convention, open the way to international arbitration for disputes arising under the foreign investment law, preferably by providing access to ICSID. (Such "ICSID clauses" are now included in the investment laws of more than 30 countries).

Investment Liberalisation

While access of foreign investors to the Ukrainian market had previously been subject to numerous restrictions, it has been considerably liberalised in recent years. Limitations remain in certain sectors, notably insurance, television and broadcasting. In the telecommunications sector, the most serious limitation applicable to foreign investors, namely the restriction on the allowed share of foreign investment in each telecommunication company, was lifted in August 2000 by the Law on "Specifics of Privatisation of Open Joint Stock Company 'Uktelecom'". Foreign investors are still not allowed to own land, and they have been able to participate in privatisations in a few cases only.

It is recommended that the remaining cases of foreign investor discrimination be reviewed with a view to eliminating them wherever feasible.

Incentives and Privileges

While the first generation of post-independence legislation provided generous incentives to foreign investments (especially tax holidays), most of them have been phased out since 1996. An exemption from import duties and import taxes of capital goods imported as contributions in kind into the charter fund of a foreign investment enterprise is the most important remaining privilege of foreign investors. The stated policy of Ukraine is now in favour of creating "level playing fields" where all investors in the Ukrainian market are treated equally, regardless of their origin.

This policy must be applauded, because no distinction in the treatment of domestic and foreign investors is justified. International experience suggests that investment incentives tend to mobilise less additional investment than governments usually expect. Frequently, they distort competition between domestic and foreign-owned enterprises as well as among foreign investors. They tend to foster corruption, especially if granted on a case-by-case basis. As a rule, the economic costs associated with incentives exceed the gains from mobilising additional investment. It is therefore advisable to phase out all remaining incentive schemes to the extent that they distinguish between foreign and domestic investors. Once granted, however, privileges should be maintained for the entire time period initially established; a retroactive repeal is likely to undermine confidence in the reliability of investment conditions.

Special Economic Zones

Some 21 special economic zones ("SEZs") or priority development areas ("PDAs") have been set up to encourage investment in less developed regions. Investors, domestic and foreign, in such zones are granted considerable fiscal benefits. Admission to these zones is usually limited to large investments; and enterprises within the zones are subject to tight state regulation and control. As a result of criticism from the IMF and the EU, the creation of new zones has been suspended until 2003.

The present regime of highly regulated SEZs relying on fiscal privileges to attract investments appears to do more harm than good to economic recovery. The mobilisation of investment into some SEZs might come at the expense of investment which otherwise would have taken place elsewhere in Ukraine. In this case, budgetary costs have been incurred through granting fiscal privileges without adding value to Ukraine's economy. More important than the direct fiscal costs are the indirect economic costs as a result of distorted competition.

The focus of SEZs on large investors, together with non-transparent administrative procedures, prevents competition within the SEZs; and the privileges granted to quasi-monopolists within the zones distorts competition to the detriment of enterprises outside the zones. It is therefore advisable to review the concept of SEZs with a view to abandoning plans for the creation of new zones and to phasing out of existing ones. Incentives already granted to enterprises in the zone should be honoured, however, to avoid undermining investor confidence in the stability of investment conditions.

Foreign Investment Institutions

While the legal framework for FDI appears to be compatible with that in eastern European transition economies, implementing institutions in Ukraine are widely rated as ineffective. Until the end of 1999, relevant responsibilities were dispersed among several institutions on the central, provincial (*oblast*) and local levels, without clear demarcation lines and accountabilities. To correct this, in early 2000 four central government agencies with FDI-related responsibilities were integrated into the Ministry of Economy and one agency was abolished. This concentration of FDI expertise now offers an opportunity for a coherent and consistently implemented investment promotion strategy.

Such a strategy would include the following tasks:

- developing a coherent investment promotion strategy to which all Ukrainian authorities subscribe;
- simplifying interaction between foreign investors and Ukrainian authorities by considering the creation, for instance, of a "one-stop shop" that obtains for foreign investors all required licenses, approvals and permits from the authorities in charge;
- assisting foreign investors in case of difficulties with Ukrainian authorities;
- facilitating an ongoing and systematic policy dialogue between foreign investors in Ukraine and investment policy-makers;
- enhancing both Ukraine's image abroad as an attractive investment location and the image of foreign investment in Ukraine as an agent of growth;
- promoting abroad investment projects in Ukraine; and
- promoting linkages between foreign investors and domestic suppliers.

In many transition economies, investment promotion agencies have been created to carry out the above-mentioned functions. These agencies should ideally:

- have an autonomous status detached from government bureaucracy;
- have a managerial structure similar to a private corporation, typically with a managing board comprising representatives of both public and private sectors;
- adopt a remuneration and incentive system competitive with the private sector;
- focus solely on investment promotion;
- enjoy the support of, and have direct access to, the political leadership; and
- derive their status and powers directly from enabling legislation, most suitably from the Foreign Investment Law.

While such agencies reportedly operate successfully in some transition economies (e.g. Poland, Hungary, and Bulgaria), the creation of such an agency in Ukraine might:

- be very difficult to implement in practice because there are separate laws regulating various types of business activity and requiring certain types of permits or licenses within certain sectors;[3]
- lead to increased government bureaucracy;
- run counter to the aim of concentrating investment promotion responsibilities in one institution (i.e. the Ministry of Economy); and
- stifle local initiatives if the agency attempts to exercise control over them.

Indeed, there was a prototype of "one-stop-agency" (not actually issuing permits and licenses, but facilitating this process) before in Ukraine, the National Agency for Reconstruction and Development, but it was not able to achieve much progress in encouraging foreign investment. The Government is now reviewing the concept and requested OECD's assistance to benefit the experience of successful agencies with a view to determining how investment promotion activities could best be organised in the Ukrainian context.

In April 1997 a Foreign Investment Advisory Council (FIAC) was established under the chairmanship of the President of Ukraine as a forum for an ongoing policy dialogue between the chief Ukrainian economic policy-makers and senior foreign executives of large multinational enterprises. Thus far the Council has met three times; and some of its recommendations have been implemented.

To strengthen the effectiveness of the Council, it is recommended to create a permanent working body to prepare and provide follow-up to Council meetings.

Such a body could comprise the top aides of Ukrainian Council members and the chief resident representatives of international Council members. It is furthermore proposed to invite into the Council membership some representatives of business associations so as to address the particular interests and problems of small and medium-sized enterprises ("SMEs").

Also in 1997 a Chamber of Independent Experts was created to arbitrate disputes between foreign investors and Ukrainian authorities. While its conclusions are not binding on the parties, they are submitted directly to the President of Ukraine for a final decision. Thus far, the Chamber has considered some 10 cases and in most instances its findings were voluntarily agreed by the parties.

The Chamber provides some protection against state authorities, especially insofar as no administrative courts have been created (see below). Its credibility depends on the attention that the President of Ukraine gives to its conclusions. To enhance the Chamber's effectiveness, it could be considered to:

- create specialised panels, notably on tax and customs issues;
- extend the Chamber's jurisdiction to enterprises with foreign shareholders (rather than just foreign shareholders in such enterprises); and
- appoint individual experts as mediators of evolving disputes before constituting formal panels.

Rule of Law System

Substantive law

One of the most important issues to improve foreign investment is the reliability of the administrative and judicial system. The lack of a strong tradition of independence and impartiality within the judiciary makes it even more important that the basic structures of the judicial system be strengthened to ensure a strong judicial power that would provide an effective and full guarantee to the protection of fundamental rights and freedoms.

There exists a vast body of law in Ukraine, but a coherent, effective and transparent legal system is still lacking. As a result, business operators spend considerable resources on complying with a myriad of legal regulations, but still face uncertainties and inadequate protection of their property rights and contracts. Three main reasons account for the inadequacy of the legal system in Ukraine:

- Soviet law is still in force unless it has been repealed or superseded by post-independence Ukrainian legislation. Furthermore, the quality of new post-independence legislation in Ukraine is in some cases not better than the Soviet legislation. Among many reasons for the sometimes poor quality

19

of current legislation is often incompetent legislative drafting, absence of co-ordination among various executive bodies responsible for legislative drafting, and absence of co-ordination within the Supreme *Rada* (Parliament).

- Many laws simply state general principles to be specified in secondary legislation and administrative instructions, and the latter are normally not publicly available.

- Most post-independence legislation has been adopted piecemeal to transform specific policy measures into law, without due regard to the coherence of the legal system. Gaps and inconsistencies among individual clauses are the consequence.

Thus far, only one major system-building codification has been adopted: the Constitution of June 1996. All other fundamental codifications are still pending in Parliament or even still under preparation, including:

- comprehensive civil code awaiting adoption since its introduction nine years ago (at present the Soviet civil code of 1963 is still in force);

- comprehensive tax code;

- law on the judiciary system;

- law on administrative procedures; and

- new rules of civil, administrative and, possibly, commercial procedure.

The civil code, inspired by the German and Dutch civil codes, is designed to set out the basic concepts and terminology for the entire private law system. It is therefore recommended to:

- adopt the pending draft civil code as soon as possible; and

- during the period prior to adoption of the code, base specific legislation (*e.g.* company legislation, secured transactions) on the pertinent provisions of the draft civil code.

Judiciary

The court system comprises the constitutional court, the "courts of general jurisdiction" and the "*arbitrazh* courts". The latter are in charge of "economic" disputes, *i.e.* disputes between enterprises, between enterprises and state authorities, and bankruptcy cases. Judicial protection against state authorities was introduced in 1996. While there are three levels of general courts (first instance, appeals, Supreme Court), there are only two levels of *arbitrazh* courts (first instance and Supreme Court).

Effective court protection requires improvements with respect to:

- technical and financial resources of the courts; and

- competency of judges, especially in economic matters.

Until recently, the execution of court decisions involved overly lengthy procedures, and one third of awards was reportedly not executed at all. In 1998 a new enforcement system was set up under the Ministry of Justice.

At present, legislation for a comprehensive reorganisation of the court system is pending in Parliament. According to the Constitution, the new system must be in place by June 2001.

It is recommended to:

- strengthen the institutional capacity of the judiciary and in particular enhance the competency of judges on commercial issues;

- proceed as expeditiously as possible with the reorganisation of the court system and the adoption of new rules of procedure;

- establish courts of appeal for economic disputes;

- explore the feasibility of some specialisation of judges by creating either specialised courts or specialised chambers within the courts. Such specialisation should especially be considered with respect to intellectual property, taxation and bankruptcy cases; and

- create an effective system of preliminary protection of creditors' rights and preliminary protection against illegal action or inaction of state authorities.

Company Law

Business enterprises are regulated by two 1991 laws, namely the Law on Enterprises and the Law on Companies. Progressive when adopted, this legislation contains major weaknesses relating to:

- protection of (minority) shareholders against insider dealing, asset stripping, profit skimming, share dilution, and other malpractices;

- unnecessary restrictions imposed on corporate finance;

- lack of transparency (no company register).

A new draft law on joint stock companies, which takes into account the draft model law for CIS countries and "General Principles of Company Law in Transition Economies",[4] is expected to be submitted to Parliament shortly.

Ukraine's present company legislation appears to be inadequate by international standards; and the duality of the Law on Enterprises and the Law on Companies creates unnecessary complexity and confusion. It is recommended to develop entirely new legislation for various types of businesses based on relevant provisions of the draft civil code. Before preparing drafts, a decision should be taken as to whether all types of businesses should be covered in one comprehensive codification or whether separate laws should be envisaged for

21

different types. Proper consideration should be given to the above-mentioned draft on joint stock companies.

The new legislation should in particular strengthen shareholders' protection through appropriate provisions on management responsibilities, equal treatment of shareholders as well as provisions against conflicts of interest on the part of corporate managers, supervisors and majority shareholders (insider dealing and insider trading). Rules concerning fiduciary duties of corporate officials should also be developed. The restrictions on corporate finance should be reviewed in the light of international practice.

The OECD Principles of Corporate Governance[5] could provide an appropriate starting point for developing modern Ukrainian company legislation. In addition, the draft CIS model laws on joint stock companies and limited liability companies, as well as the "General Principles of Company Law in Transition Economies", could be taken into consideration.

It is furthermore recommended to create a company register in line with common practice in western market economies. The register could be based on the First European Community Company Law Directive.

Taxation

Taxation tops the list of investment disincentives in Ukraine and drives an increasing number of domestic business operators into the shadow economy. Investors complain about:

- the high effective level of taxes due to restrictions on depreciation allowances, the deductibility of bad debts, and the deductibility of business expenses (even though tax rates as such are relatively moderate);

- the ambiguity and inconsistency of tax legislation, which prevents taxpayers from fully complying with the law and also results in costly and needless disputes between taxpayers and tax authorities.

- burdensome compliance requirements, including the quarterly filing of profit tax declarations and the monthly computation of profit by enterprises.

- the number of taxes, as there exist over 30 different types of taxes , of which six account for more than 80 per cent of state revenues;

- frequent changes in tax legislation and reporting requirements;

- arbitrary and opaque tax administration, especially the imposition of fines disproportionate to the gravity of the violation.

Nevertheless, improvements in the tax system in recent years must be recognised, notably:

- the right of tax authorities to retain 30 per cent of all fines collected was repealed in 1999;

- in early 2001 the power of tax authorities to unilaterally withdraw amounts from a taxpayer's bank account in order to pay taxes (*kartoteka*) was abolished and was replaced by a system that generally requires the tax authorities to notify taxpayers of taxes that are due and that provides taxpayers the opportunity to appeal tax determinations to a court and to arrange for the deferred payment of taxes; and

- double taxation agreements were concluded with some 30 countries.

In the summer of 2000 Parliament approved in the first reading a new tax code which would consolidate all Ukrainian taxes in a single document, decrease the number of taxes, reduce the rates for the VAT, enterprise profit tax, and personal income tax, reduce the reporting burden for enterprises, and codify simplified taxation procedures for SMEs.

The adoption of a tax code that is comprehensive, coherent, and consistent with international standards would significantly improve the tax system in Ukraine and would facilitate investment in Ukraine. The decrease in the number of taxes, the reduction in the reporting burden for enterprises and the simplified procedures for SMEs would also contribute to a more favourable investment environment in Ukraine. However, to address the main points of criticism of the present tax system, it is important that the tax code be amended to:

- improve the language of the law to eliminate numerous inconsistencies and ambiguities;

- follow international standards concerning the deductibility of business expenses, the determination of depreciation allowances, and the rules of accounting for income and expenses; and

- rationalise the system of penalties so that the amount of the penalty bears a closer correspondence to the gravity of the taxpayer's violation.

It is recommended that prior to the adoption of a new tax code no new legislation should be enacted that would increase the tax liability of enterprises or investors.

It is further recommended to establish tax ombudsman offices staffed with tax experts who would provide assistance to businesses in filing their tax declarations and in resolving problems that businesses may encounter in their dealings with the tax authorities. Tax authorities should also be authorised to issue written interpretations of the law to taxpayers, which would binding on the tax authorities.

Property Protection and Secured Lending

Ownership system

Even though in principle recognised by the Ukrainian Constitution, private ownership of land is in practice still restricted to plots for residence and agricultural subsistence. For business purposes, land can only be leased (for a maximum period of 98 years). Under the 1992 Land Code, foreigners are expressly prohibited from owning land. However, in April 2000 the Cabinet approved a new draft land code for submission to Parliament. This draft envisages private ownership of land for both industrial and agricultural purposes, and it would allow foreigners to acquire non-arable land in urban areas for industrial purposes (thus limiting the discrimination against foreigners to agricultural plot ownership).

It is recommended to proceed with the adoption of a new land code that would liberalise private ownership of land for all purposes. Foreigners should be able to own land on the same conditions as Ukrainian citizens ("National Treatment").

Intellectual Property Protection

In theory, intellectual property rights are protected in Ukraine under both domestic legislation and pertinent international treaties to which Ukraine has acceded, particularly for industrial property protection (patents, trademarks, etc) and, to some extent, authors' rights. In practice, however, infringements abound, with a piracy rate for computer software estimated at some 95 per cent of the output.

The protection of intellectual property needs to be enhanced in accordance with the WTO "Agreement on Trade Related Aspects of Intellectual Property Rights" (TRIPS); notably, enforcement needs to be strengthened urgently. To this end, it is recommended to:

- enhance investigative powers and administrative capacities of enforcement authorities;
- increase fines for intellectual property violations;
- increase the compensation to infringed parties;
- authorise the preliminary seizure of unauthorised products by the courts; and
- develop specialised expertise within the court system, possibly by creating a special chamber for intellectual and industrial property violations.

Secured lending

While the legislation on pledging securities is fairly appropriate and a state-of-the art "securities pledge registry" was created in 1999, adequate legislation and a title registry for mortgages are still unachieved. Thus, mortgage-based lending remains underdeveloped and local currency credits in spring 2000 ran at some 50 per cent interest and were usually available for short term only (up to one year). The adoption of relevant legislation has hitherto fallen prey to the controversy on private land ownership. At present, two interconnected draft bills pending in Parliament would create a mortgage system and a title registry for real property.

Recognition of private land ownership and development of a mortgage and title registration system for real assets are essential to developing a functioning commercial credit system in Ukraine. Pending efforts in this direction therefore deserve support. The successful creation of the pledge register for securities demonstrates that a similar system should be feasible for real property.

Creation of such a system would provide the basis for mortgage banking that could facilitate both corporate financing and financing of private housing. It could in particular foster long-term lending and drive interest rates down. Foreign investors would be able to leverage their capital transfers to Ukraine by raising additional domestic funds and would thus find investment conditions in Ukraine more attractive.

To achieve these results, however, the present "crowding out" of private borrowing by the public treasury must be ended. The creation of the legal underpinnings for a functioning credit market must go hand in hand with a reduction of the government deficit. The reduction of the deficit in the budget for 2000 marks a promising step in this direction.

Financial Sector

The government recently created a Co-ordinating Council on Financial Sector Policy, comprising all Ministers and heads of national and State Committees dealing with Economy, Finance, Taxation, Capital Markets to develop coherent national policies on financial institutions and services. This was considered commendable and advisable under prevailing circumstances when there has been a paucity of credit and investment resources, especially from abroad.

Ukraine's banking system and capital market are both still in an embryonic stage. Nevertheless, reforms aimed at the creation of a viable banking system and capital market are proceeding, some with noticeable success.

Banking

Ukraine has a two-tier banking system, which distinguishes Central Bank activity from commercial bank functions.

Central Bank functions – monetary policy and banking supervision – are vested in the National Bank of Ukraine (the "NBU"). The NBU has been relatively successful in approaching monetary stability and has recently tightened banking supervision in line with international (BIS) standards. The Law on the NBU of May 1999, while stating the NBU's independence, created a "Council of the NBU" comprised of representatives of political constituencies and endowed with policy-making powers. Amendments were made in July 2000 to the NBU Law, which weakened the authority of the Council over the NBU.

At present of the 156 banks operating in Ukraine there are only two state-owned banks and three formerly state-owned banks, with the state-owned banks accounting for about half of total turnover. While marginally effective in facilitating payments, they play only a modest role as intermediaries of savings. Confidence in the banking sector has been eroded by several failures. In January 2001, a Law on "Banks and Banking" entered into force. The Law has established clear rules for all banks and banking activities, in particular eliminating discrimination of foreign banks. Legislation on bankruptcy proceedings for insolvent banks is under preparation.

In March 2001, only six foreign banks were operating in Ukraine. Since 1997, restrictions on foreign banks were mostly lifted, even though some still remain and have even been reconfirmed in the above-mentioned bill.

It is recommended to:

- consider confining the "Council of the NBU" to an advisory role in order to dispel doubts about the NBU's independence;
- proceed with the adoption of the law on banks and banking but review the remaining restrictions on foreign bank operations in favour of a national treatment policy;
- require audits in accordance with International Auditing Standards for all banks;
- enact legislation on the bankruptcy of banks providing effective protection of depositors;
- reconsider, for this purpose, plans of introducing a national deposit insurance system (The Law on Deposit Guarantee Fund recently passed first reading in Parliament);
- restructure the Savings Bank; and
- liquidate unhealthy banks.

Capital Market

Two market systems exist in Ukraine – traditional stock exchanges (with the Ukrainian Stock Exchange as the largest) and an alternative trading system called the "Ukrainian First Stock Trading System". Operated by the association of licensed Ukrainian securities traders, the latter provides an electronic trading information network similar to the U.S. NASDAQ. Established in July 1996, it accounts for almost 90 per cent of the entire Ukrainian securities market. State oversight of the capital market is exercised by the State Commission for Securities and Stock Markets created in 1995.

While progress has been achieved in developing a functioning capital market (especially with the creation of the First Stock Trading System), further legislation will be needed to clearly define the fiduciary duties of financial intermediaries (especially investment funds, investment companies and securities traders) and to ensure proper enforcement of these duties. The self-regulatory system of securities traders should be strengthened with a view to raising professional standards. The number of trading systems could be reduced and in order to consolidate the market.

Accounting and Auditing

In August 1999, the previous Soviet-style accounting system was replaced by a system of "Ukrainian Accounting Standards" (UAS), which are not supposed to contradict international standards. The UAS are not yet fully developed, however, and enterprises with foreign investments usually still have to operate with two accounting systems, at considerable expense and complexity in the application of double taxation issues. Only banks are required since January 1998 to report under accounting standards issued by the National Bank of Ukraine, which are largely consistent with international accounting standards. Companies are still required to produce two separate sets of accounts, one for tax purposes, the other for financial reporting.

Even though large international accounting firms are present in Ukraine, only individual auditors, foreign and local alike, licensed by the Audit Chamber of Ukraine, may conduct and sign compulsory audit reports. As most Ukrainian auditors do not use International Standards of Auditing, audited financial statements have limited international credibility.

It is recommended to:

- align speedily Ukrainian accounting and auditing standards with international practice, in particular for publicly traded companies and financial institutions (reference points are the International Accounting Standards, as developed by the International Accounting Standards Committee, and International Standards of Auditing, as developed by the International Federation of Accountants);

- modify the Ukrainian commercial chart of accounts to facilitate the application of internationally recognised accounting standards;

- ensure that financial statements are tax neutral and use a reconciliation statement to link tax computation to such financial statements; and

- implement effectively the existing 1998 Presidential Decree and the October 2000 Law on SMEs for a simplified reporting system for SMEs.

Interdependencies

It should finally be emphasised that the development of the financial sector depends largely on progress in related reform areas such as:

- privatisation, where progress on large scale privatisation would increase the volume of tradable securities;
- corporate governance, where the adequate protection of minority shareholders is *conditio sine qua non* for building investor confidence in securities markets;
- taxation, where the tax implications of secondary market transactions (capital gains) need to be clarified;
- bankruptcy, where adequate protection of investors in case of bankruptcies of custodians and financial intermediaries must be provided; and
- currency regulations, where clarifications are outstanding as to whether and to what extent currency regulations apply to the purchase of Ukrainian securities by foreign residents.

Trade and Currency Regimes

While Ukraine has liberalised in recent years its trade regime and lowered its tariffs, considerable non-tariff barriers remain, especially through the imposition of cumbersome technical standards and certification requirements.

Ukraine has concluded bilateral free trade agreements with almost all CIS countries and the three Baltic countries; it is also a partner in the 1995 CIS Free Trade Agreement. Even though not (yet) a member of the WTO, Ukraine has already subscribed to most WTO disciplines in relation to the EU under its 1998 Partnership and Co-operation Agreement with the latter (although Ukraine has not bound its tariffs *vis-à-vis* the EU). At present, Ukraine actively pursues WTO membership, but must still implement a host of reforms to qualify. Following WTO accession, Ukraine intends to form a free trade area with the EU (feasibility studies under way) and to join the Central European Free Trade Agreement (CEFTA). Ukraine is moreover an active member of the Black Sea Economic Co-operation, which is envisaged to be developed into a free trade area among Black Sea countries.

Ukraine's currency regime has been largely liberalised in recent years. The *hryvnya*, the national currency, is convertible in accordance with Article VIII of the IMF Agreement. Its rate is determined freely on the Ukrainian Interbank Currency Market. Foreign investors are guaranteed the free transfer of dividends and other investment proceeds. In response to the 1998 Russian financial crisis, some regulations were introduced, notably a requirement to surrender 50 per cent of export proceeds to the NBU.

It is recommended that Ukraine:

• adopt and implement international trade policy disciplines and commitments, which would facilitate its accession to the World Trade Organisation;

• remove remaining non-tariff trade barriers and, especially, bring its technical standards and certification procedures into conformity with international practice; and

• review the suitability of its currency regulations, notably the exports proceeds surrender requirement.

Privatisation and Enterprise Reorganisation

By the end of 1998, some 80-90 per cent of state-owned enterprises had been privatised, mainly through management/employee buyout schemes and voucher/mass privatisation programmes. Foreign investors were involved in only a few cases. However, some 200 large enterprises holding over 80 per cent of assets in the industrial and utilities sectors remain state-owned. These enterprises are at the core of the government's privatisation programme for 2000-2002, even though several enterprises are "reserved" for continued state ownership. Unlike previous privatisation rounds, the 2000-2002 programme targets primarily long-term strategic investors and foreign investors in particular. To attract them, it is envisaged to reorganise enterprises earmarked for privatisation and to restructure their debt.

The objectives and tenets of the 2000-2002 programme are commendable. To achieve them, it is recommended to:[6]

• expand the list of privatisable large-scale enterprises, especially extending privatisation to energy and telecommunications (taking into account developments in OECD market economies);

• develop a transparent, predictable, methodical and stable process for case-by-case privatisation;

• establish clear qualification requirements for the selection of privatisation advisers;

• announce publicly the planned privatisations well in advance, and provide full information on the financial situation of the enterprises concerned;

• offer equal participation conditions for all parties concerned that cannot be changed after such an announcement;

29

- ensure that the tender commission should be independent with no interference in the commission's activity unless otherwise stipulated by the current legislation; and

- ensure that there must be no investment requests prior to the sale.

Bankruptcy Legislation

Privatisation of Ukrainian state enterprises regularly presupposes their reorganisation and the liquidation of pre-existing debt. With a view to facilitating this process, a new bankruptcy law entered into force in January 2000 allowing debtors to initiate bankruptcy/reorganisation procedures and making reorganisation the first choice, with liquidation the last resort. Effective bankruptcy proceedings are also urgently needed to enforce payment discipline and impose hard budget constraints on enterprise management.

While the new law marks considerable progress, its effectiveness is hampered by remaining rigidities regarding the initiation of proceedings and, especially, by lack of expertise on the part of courts entrusted with the administration of proceedings. It is recommended to:

- simplify the initiation of bankruptcy proceedings to the extent possible by all parties and, in particular, lift the requirement that creditors must have their claims confirmed by a court decision before filing for bankruptcy, even if their claims are undisputed or otherwise obvious;

- launch comprehensive training programmes for bankruptcy judges and trustees in bankruptcy; and

- enhance the abilities of bankruptcy judges in handling intricate business processes and protecting creditor and shareholder interests, perhaps by creating a centralised pool of specialised bankruptcy judges and assigning complex bankruptcy/ reorganisation cases to them.

Public Governance

Structural deficiencies and pending reform programme

Public governance is still marked by especially high "state capture" (*i.e.* undue influence of vested interests on government), bureaucratic interventionism, time tax on enterprises for interacting with authorities and bribery costs (the latter estimated at some 6.5 per cent of enterprise revenues). A bloated bureaucracy with broad discretionary powers and non-transparent accountability, an under-trained and highly volatile civil service, and a still embryonic "civil society" have fostered Ukraine's development towards "crony capitalism". To rectify this situation, the government, with parliamentary endorsement, adopted in spring 2000 a five-year programme aimed at developing human resources, alleviating poverty, increasing competitiveness of the Ukrainian economy, protecting human rights and freedoms, and promoting Ukraine's integration into the European Union.

As a first step in the implementation of this programme, the government has started to downsize the government apparatus and refocus it from micro-managing the economy towards creating and ensuring framework conditions for market operations. It has also taken initiatives to reduce barter settlements in transactions involving the public sector.

Through the creation of the State Committee for Regulatory Policy and Entrepreneurial Activity (SCRPEA) and its significant strengthening in 2000, the government is actively and systematically proceeding with deregulation efforts, as well as "filtering" proposed new regulations. For instance, between 1 January and 31 December 2000, the SCRPEA reviewed and made decisions to revoke or amend 136 existing regulations. On a cumulative basis, 71% of all cases SCRPEA was successful in challenging regulations (69 regulations have been fully deregulated or repealed, 27 regulations have been partially deregulated or amended. In the current quarter, 52% of draft regulations reviewed were not approved by SCRPEA and returned to the promulgating agency for further work and amendment.

Business regulations

Until 1997, excessive licensing requirements, together with lengthy and cumbersome procedures, constituted formidable business entry barriers, especially for SMEs. A reduction of these requirements and simplification of procedures in 1997-98 brought significant progress, even though remarkable differences in the time required to complete registration among regions suggest that further improvements are possible.

Also, until 1997, business operations were interrupted and sometimes definitely frustrated by frequent inspections by tax and other authorities. In response to a presidential decree restraining authorities' inspection rights, both the number and duration of inspections of SMEs fell sharply in 1998. However, it increased again slightly in 1999 (albeit not to previous levels).

The new law On Licensing Certain Types of Entrepreneurial Activity was passed by Parliament in final reading on 1 June 2000 and signed by the President on 2 July 2000. The new law eliminates satisfying technical requirements as a pre-condition to issuance of a license, and all procedures are more clear and transparent. According to the new law all licensing requirements (specific regulations) must pass regulatory expertise in SCRPEA before adopted. Adoption of the new Law reduced the number of activities to be licensed from 100+ (including sub-activities) to 60. Such activities as beer brewing, auditing, practice of law, general tourist and recreation business and others were eliminated. No new activities were added."

A Presidential Decree of 22 January 2000 on "Introduction of a Uniform State Regulatory Policy in the Sphere of Entrepreneurship" states that establishing a uniform state policy favouring entrepreneurship is one of the primary objectives of the government, and sets forth five principles for regulatory policy:

   i) demonstration of necessity for government regulation

   ii) demonstration that proposed regulations will achieve the desired result

   iii) consistency and co-ordination of regulations

   iv) publicity and public input in the regulatory process, and

   v) transparency.

Competition

Ukraine has relatively advanced competition/antimonopoly legislation enforced by the Antimonopoly Commission and the *arbitrazh* courts. Nevertheless, competition remains distorted due to the subsidisation of preferred enterprises and a significant shadow economy.

While previously high direct subsidies (15 per cent of GDP in 1991) have come down to acceptable levels (2.2 per cent of GDP in 1998), indirect subsidies in the form of tax preferences, selective non-enforcement of arrears on taxes, social security and other fiscal charges (such arrears amounting to 12.7 per cent in 1998), tax write-offs and tax restructuring, targeted credits and government guarantees, and the granting of monopoly rights exceed international levels by far. To an increasing extent, tax and customs privileges granted to enterprises in special economic zones also distort competition.

The system of Government guarantees for credits obtained in hard currency from foreign lenders by Ukrainian companies needs to be eliminated as soon as possible. This system encourages serious corruption, causes unfair competition and already resulted in tremendous losses for the state budget since most of the companies failed to repay their credits and the Government had to pay them out of the state budget.

Subsidisation practices are not transparent, giving rise to concerns about excessive bureaucracy and corruption. Steps have been taken, however, to drastically reduce subsidies. Thus, in May 2000 the tax privileges of some 150 state enterprises were annulled.

Competition is highly distorted by the shadow economy (some 50-70 per cent of GDP) since enterprises in the shadow enjoy *de facto* exemption from taxation, social contributions and government regulations.

Recommendations

While public governance in Ukraine is still regarded as problematic, decisive reforms are pending and have already shown results in some areas. The reform agenda included in the government's present five-year programme merits support. To create an investor-friendly climate, reforms must:

- reorient government bureaucracy from micro-managing the economy to the strategic formulation of framework conditions conducive to private sector development;

- restructure government bureaucracy with a view to enhancing efficiency, transparency, accountability, predictability and integrity;

- develop the legal system and, above all, put in place an institutional infrastructure with a view to ensuring effective and consistent protection of contracts and property rights as well as protection of business operators against the misuse of power on the part of public authorities;

- enforce hard budget constraints, in both the public and private sectors;

- continue with deregulating business activities, with a particular view to fostering SMEs,[7] and

- carry out and expand the envisaged privatisation of large state enterprises.

Competition /antimonopoly law and policy are vital to promoting investment and to the entire reform process. It is therefore encouraging that the Antimonopoly Committee (AMC) has not been subjected to the downsizing process. Indeed, OECD studies indicate that competition/antimonopoly authorities have been important not only through their law enforcement activities but also as advocates of the kind of market-oriented regulatory reform that is needed in Ukraine. It is recommended that Ukraine consider making greater use of the AMC for advice on the harm to Ukrainian consumers from existing and proposed subsidies and regulatory policies, including those relating to privatisation and regulation of enterprises with some "natural monopoly" component.

With a particular view to curbing corrupt practices, a government programme on building integrity of the public service is recommended. As corruption is rooted in structural deficiencies of the organisation of the Ukrainian state, such a programme cannot be successful if it focuses just on detecting and punishing wrongdoing. Rather, comprehensive reforms of the public sector are required to change incentives, capacities and attitudes of public officials. Such a programme should encompass:

- administrative law reforms introducing clear, simple and publicly available rules governing public administration and reducing officials' discretionary powers to the extent possible. The pending work on a law on administrative procedures plays a central role in this context;

- public sector reorganisation to increase transparency and accountability of officials. In this context, the powers of the State Auditing Chamber should be strengthened, and the office of an Ombudsman for Public Service Integrity could be established, possibly associated with the State Auditing Chamber;

- judicial reforms designed to enhance judicial review of misuses of power. In addition to the envisaged creation of an administrative court system, remedies for private parties could be strengthened to assert rules of fair play, including actions by non-governmental groups and associations;

- civil service reform to afford public servants an adequate remuneration and a clear career track that motivates professional behaviour;

- privatisation to remove opportunities for misallocation of public resources. It is in particular recommended to extend privatisation to the provision of infrastructure and public services wherever feasible with a view to introducing competition between public and private providers;

- measures to encourage cash transactions instead of barter trade; and

- introducing a system of codes of ethics for certain professions (*e.g.* legal, accounting professions) and business sectors (*e.g.* financial intermediaries) creating peer pressures against illicit conduct.

A free and independent press is important in helping to combat corruption and in fostering transparency within the government and in the private sector. It is finally recommended that Ukraine participate in efforts to combat bribery of foreign public officials in international business transactions in accordance with the 1997 OECD Convention.

1. Economic and Political Situation

1.1. Economic situation

Ukraine, a country with some 50 million people,[8] has sound fundamentals for attaining prosperity – a highly educated labour force, rich natural resources, a highly developed, though ailing infrastructure, a large consumer market, and a strategic location at the crossroads of Central Europe, Russia, Central Asia and the Middle East. When it gained independence in August 1991, most Ukrainian and many international observers expected rapid economic growth, leaving most other transition economies behind. However, developments have proven this expectation an illusion.

Until last year, Ukraine was the only transition economy that experienced a decline of its GDP and erosion of living standards in every year since it gained independence in 1991. By 1998, Ukraine's official GDP had plummeted to some 37 per cent of its pre-independence 1989 level.[9] During the same period, GDPs in all CIS countries shrunk to an average of 53 per cent while GDP in Poland grew to some 117 per cent of its 1990 level. In 1999, the average monthly wage in Ukraine was $47 equivalent, down from $68 in 1998 and $84 in 1997. The real average wage in 1999 was just 31 per cent of that in 1990; and more than half of the population lived below the poverty line. Although these figures probably overstate the actual decline due to deficiencies of Soviet statistics and the disregard of the shadow economy, they do indicate that living conditions of the majority of Ukrainians have deteriorated considerably since Soviet times.

The economic decline, which has been reversed last year, is also reflected in persistent fiscal and current account deficits, even though these deficits gradually decreased since 1994. The same holds true for inflation, which came down from some 10 000 per cent in 1993 amid the post-Soviet economic chaos to 19.2 per cent in 1999 and 25.8 per cent in 2000. In 2001 the government hopes to compress annual inflation to around 12 to 15 per cent.[10]

The virtual collapse of the formal economy came hand-in-glove with a steady increase of the shadow economy. The causes of the rapid development of the shadow economy in Ukraine are closely related to the dissolution of the old political and economic systems and, subsequently, to delayed economic reforms.

Table 1.   **GDP Growth (1993-2000) in Ukraine and Other Transition Economies**
%

	1993	1994	1995	1996	1997	1998	1999	2000*
Ukraine	−14.2	−22.9	−12.2	−10.0	−3.0	−1.9	−0.4	6.0
Central Europe								
Czech Republic	0.1	2.2	5.9	4.8	−1.0	−2.2	−0.2	2.5
Hungary	−0.6	2.9	1.5	1.3	4.6	4.9	4.5	5.5
Poland	3.8	5.2	7.0	6.0	6.8	4.8	4.1	5.0
Slovakia	−3.7	4.9	6.7	6.2	6.2	4.1	1.9	2.0
Slovenia	2.8	5.3	4.1	3.5	4.6	3.8	4.9	4.5
Baltics								
Estonia	−8.5	−2.0	4.3	3.9	10.6	4.7	−1.1	6.0
Latvia	−15.0	0.8	−1.0	3.3	8.6	3.9	0.1	4.0
Lithuania	−16.2	−9.8	3.3	4.7	7.3	5.1	−4.2	2.0
South East Europe								
Albania	9.6	8.3	13.3	9.1	−7.0	8.0	7.3	7.0
Bosnia and Herzegovina	n.a.	n.a.	20.8	69.0	30.0	12.4	10.0	15.0
Bulgaria	−1.5	1.8	2.9	−10.1	−7.0	3.5	2.4	5.0
Croatia	−8.0	5.9	6.8	5.9	6.8	2.5	−0.3	3.0
FYR Macedonia	−9.1	−1.8	−1.2	1.2	1.4	2.9	2.7	6.0
Romania	1.5	3.9	7.1	3.9	−6.1	−5.4	−3.2	1.5
FR Yugoslavia	n.a.	n.a.	6.1	5.9	7.4	2.5	−23.2	5.0
CIS								
Russia	−8.7	−12.7	−4.1	−3.4	0.9	−4.6	3.2	6.5
Armenia	−8.8	5.4	6.9	5.9	3.3	7.2	3.3	3.5
Azerbaijan	−23.1	−19.7	11.8	1.3	5.8	10.0	7.2	10.0
Belarus	−7.6	−12.6	−10.4	2.8	11.4	8.3	3.4	4.0
Georgia	−25.4	−11.4	2.4	10.5	10.8	2.9	3.0	4.0
Kazakhstan	−9.2	−12.6	−8.2	0.5	1.7	−1.9	1.7	10.0
Kyrgyzstan	−16.0	−20.1	−5.4	7.1	9.9	2.1	3.6	6.0
Moldova	−1.2	−31.2	−1.4	−7.8	1.3	−8.6	−4.4	−3.0
Tajikistan	−11.0	−18.9	−12.5	−4.4	1.7	5.3	3.7	4.0
Turkmenistan	−10.0	−17.3	−7.2	−6.7	−11.3	5.0	16.0	18.0
Uzbekistan	−2.3	−4.2	−0.9	1.6	2.5	4.4	4.1	1.5

*projection.
Sources: EBRD, EIU, WIIW, EU, national statistics.

The official estimates of the shadow economy by *Derzhcomstat* claim that its share is roughly 13-14 per cent of official GDP. It should be stressed that this amount is included in official estimates. However, more realistic estimates range between 50 and 70 per cent of official GDP in 2000. While the shadow economy somewhat compensates for the decline of the formal economy, it also increases distortions in the Ukrainian economy, with allegations of corruption pervading all layers of the state.

While until 1999 independent Ukraine steadily moved towards the economic abyss, the year 2000 was a turning point. In 2000, real GDP increased in year-on-

Chart 1. **GDP Growth Rates in Ukraine (1996-2001) in Real Terms**

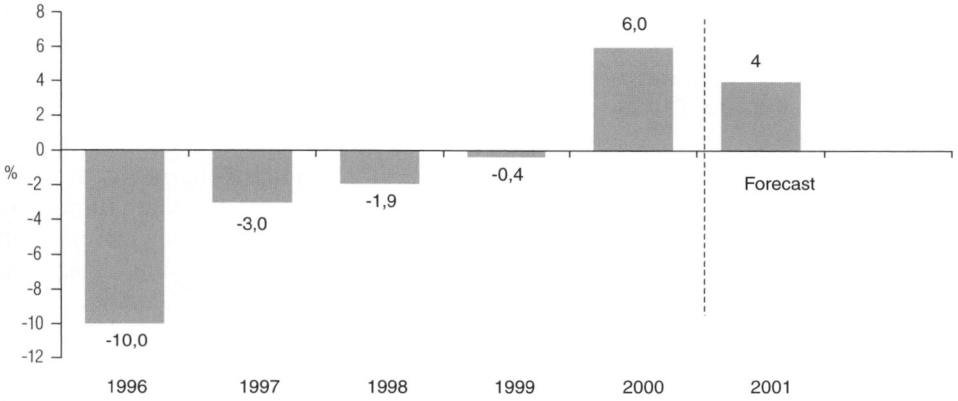

Source: Ministry of Economy, Ukraine.

Table 2. **Macroeconomic Indicators**[11]

	1994	1995	1996	1997	1998	1999
Real GDP growth	−23.0	−12.2	−10.0	−3.0	−1.7	−2.5
Inflation	401.0	181.0	39.7	10.1	20.0	17.0
Registered unemployment	0.3	0.5	1.3	2.3	3.7	..
Consolidated fiscal balance (% of GDP)	−9.1	−4.9	−3.2	−5.6	−2.7	−1.5
Primary balance (% of GDP)	−3.7	−3.4	−1.6	−3.7	−0.4	1.4
Current account (US$ bn)	−1.4	−1.5	−1.2	−1.3	−1.3	−0.3
Current account (% of GDP)	−3.7	−4.4	−2.7	−2.7	−3.0	−1.1

year terms by 6 per cent. Export revenues surged to $13.3 billion in 2000, while imports were at $14 billion. Ukraine posted its first trade surplus in five years in 2000, exporting $616 million more than it imported. Russia continued to be the country's largest single trading partner. Russia is the largest consumer of Ukrainian exports. Turkey replaced China as the number two export recipient, followed by Germany, US and Italy. Top five sources of imports are Russia, Germany, Turkmenistan, Belarus and Kazakhstan, according to the State Statistical Bureau. The Government successfully renegotiated its foreign debt of $12.5 billion.[12] For the first time since independence, a relatively balanced budget was adopted, with a deficit of some 1.5-2.0 per cent of GDP (if the IMF methodology is used).

Ukraine plays a crucial role in regional energy diplomacy as a large energy importer and a major transhipment route from Russia to Europe. It is the main

37

export route for Russian gas to the European market, and pipelines carrying Russian oil for export through its Black Sea ports cross Ukrainian territory. Oil transit is likely to decrease, as Russia finds alternative outlets for its oil, including the construction of a new pipeline designed to bypass Ukraine. On the other hand, Ukraine would benefit from any oil pipeline that were designed to carry Caspian oil directly to Europe. The most important pipelines are however those that carry the natural gas.

Although oil and gas pipelines are an important source of earnings, there is some concern about the serviceability of this ageing infrastructure. Under an agreement with the Russian supplier Gazprom the transit fees are in fact paid in natural gas. Gazprom also contests that a very substantial amount of its gas unaccountably "leaks" from the pipeline during its transit through Ukraine.

1.2. Political Environment

Ukraine is a central state comprising 24 provinces (or *oblast*), two cities (Kiev and Sevastopol) with the status of a province and the Crimean Autonomous Republic. Under Ukraine's 1996 Constitution, power has been formally divided among three branches of state power – the executive, the legislature, and the judiciary. Although the Constitution has not definitively resolved the formal division of powers among the three branches, it has provided the Ukrainians with a strong legal framework for addressing this problem. More importantly, it has codified the fundamental rights of free speech, freedom of the press and assembly, and freedom of religion for all Ukrainians.

The President is the pre-eminent figure in the power structure, even though his constitutional powers are less strong than those of his Russian counterpart. The President appoints and dismisses the Prime Minister (appointment subject to parliamentary approval), is the commander-in-chief of the armed forces and may initiate and veto legislation.

The Government is headed by the Prime Minister. In early 2000, it launched a comprehensive reform of the Government structure, considerably downsizing the apparatus. In practice, Government competencies are shared with a sizeable and powerful Presidential Administration.

Ukraine's unicameral Parliament, known as the Verkhovna Rada, is elected for a four-year term. The 450-member Parliament adopts legislation, ratifies international agreements, and approves the budget. Beginning with the 29 March 1998 elections, half of the Supreme Rada's seats are filled from individual single-seat districts, while the other half are filled from political party lists. Each citizen would cast two national votes – one under each system. Until the end of 1999, the leftist factions of the Rada, with the support of sympathising independent deputies, managed to block most reform legislation. In spring 2000, strengthened by by-elections in June 2000, a new pro-Presidential majority was constituted, offering for the first time an opportunity for co-operation between President, Government and Parliament in the pursuit of reforms. This facilitated the parliamentary endorsement of a Government-proposed five-year reform strategy for 2000-2005, the adoption of a low-deficit budget for 2000, and the above-mentioned reforms of the Government apparatus. The next parliamentary elections are due in March 2002.

Ukraine's foreign economic policy tries to reconcile Ukraine's continued dependence on Russia (20 per cent of exports, 47 per cent of imports, notably energy, and large debt arrears) with its emphasis on independence and its desire for rapprochement with the EU. Against this background, Ukraine has concluded free trade agreements with all CIS countries, actively promotes economic co-operation within the framework of the Black Sea Economic Co-operation (BSEC), hopes to join the World Trade Organisation, has concluded a Partnership and Co-operation Agreement with the EU, endeavours to accede to the Central European Free Trade Agreement (CEFTA) and eventually to form a free trade area with the EU. At its summit meeting in Helsinki in December 1999, the European Council adopted a "Common Strategy of the European Union on Ukraine" emphasising the EU's support for the democratic and economic reform process in Ukraine, and "strengthening co-operation between the EU and Ukraine within the context of EU enlargement".

IMF, World Bank and EBRD have programmes for and representative offices in Ukraine. In 1999, the IMF had suspended disbursements on a $2.6 bn Extended Fund Facility loan programme upon realising that the National Bank of Ukraine) in 1997-98 had overstated its foreign reserves in order to qualify for further *tranches* of lending. In September 2000, this issue was settled and one *tranche* of about $245 million was disbursed in December 2000. The World Bank has committed $2.2 billion to twelve projects, with a further $200 million in guarantees. However, disbursements under the Electricity Market Development Loan and Agricultural Sector Adjustment Loan have been suspended as a result of the failure by the Ukrainian authorities to implement benchmarked reforms.

On 12 September 2000, the World Bank announced a new three-year $1.8 billion lending programme to replace the earlier one in effect since 1996, together with a new country strategy on Ukraine.[13] Like the IMF, the World Bank has expressed concerns that Ukraine's tenuous recovery could prove short-lived without further progress on land privatisation, large-scale cash sell-offs of state enterprises and energy sector reorganisation. The effectiveness of previous World Bank lending has suffered as a result of lengthy delays and poor implementation, stemming from Ukraine's ineffective policy-formulating environment, widespread corruption and opposition from Parliament.

At the end of 1999 the EBRD had 30 projects in Ukraine worth a total of EUR 809 million, of which a little under two-thirds were in the private sector. The

EU provided macro-financial assistance to Ukraine in the past, but its support has now focused more in the areas of justice and home affairs. It also provides technical assistance within the framework of the TACIS-programme in developing a transparent and stable legal, regulatory and institutional framework, and supporting the development of the health system. Several OECD member countries operate technical assistance programmes in Ukraine, with the USAID being by far the largest.

2. Foreign Investment Trends and Investment Climate

2.1. Statistics

As of the 1st January 2001, total foreign direct investment (FDI) in Ukraine has accumulated to some $3.9 billion since independence. This translated into some $79 per capita, placing Ukraine the second lowest among CIS countries, ahead of Belarus only; and it is less than 10 per cent of per capita FDI to Central and Eastern European countries, such as Poland and Hungary.

Chart 2. **Top Ten FDI Destinations in Central Europe, 1990-2000**

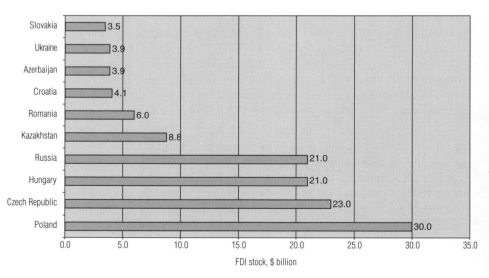

FDI stock, $ billion

* Projection
Source: Business Central Europe, The Annual 2001.

While foreign investment into the Ukraine remains marginal, capital flight from the Ukraine since 1991 is estimated to accumulate to some 20 billion. At a time when Ukraine urgently needs fresh capital injections into its ailing industrial infrastructure, it has become in fact a capital exporting country, mainly to offshore centres.

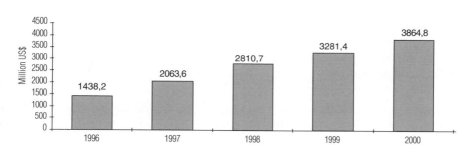

Chart 3. **FDI Inflow to Ukraine (1996-2000)**
Million US$

Source: Ministry of Economy, Ukraine

FDI in Ukraine is not only marginal, but also highly concentrated on a few regions, as is the case in most other emerging/transition economies. Kiev and its surroundings received over one-third of all FDI; Donetsk, Zaporozhye, Poltava, Odessa and Dnipropetrovsk regions together accumulated another third; leaving less than one-third for the remainder of the country. By origin of investment, the United States has been the dominant foreign investor. United States companies have made investments valued at some $590 million, representing 18 per cent of all FDI made in Ukraine. The United States is followed by the Netherlands with 9 per cent, the Russian Federation (9 per cent), Germany (7 per cent) and the United Kingdom (7 per cent).

From a sector perspective, as of January 2000, the main destination of FDI in Ukraine, was the domestic food industry[14] (20 per cent of cumulative FDI), followed by domestic commercial operations (over 17 per cent) and mechanical engineering/metals (almost 11 per cent). Other promising sectors for foreign investment include: energy,[15] building materials,[16] consumer goods, information and communications technologies,[17] health care, transportation, environmental technologies, and tourism.

2.2. Investment Climate Surveys

The failure to attract foreign investment, staggering capital flight, the collapse of the formal economy and the relative growth of the shadow economy are in sharp contrast to the solid fundamentals of Ukraine such as a well educated and skilled labour force (98.6 per cent literacy rate), an extensive though ailing infrastructure, fertile soil and a strategic location between Asian and European markets. In fact, most Ukrainians' expectations in 1991 for rapid improvement in their living standards were to some extent shared by Western experts.

The economic decline of Ukraine since the onset of independence cannot be attributed only to economic fundamentals. They are mainly due to exceptionally difficult conditions for business activities in Ukraine that deter investors, domestic and foreign alike, drive Ukrainian entrepreneurs underground and encourage Ukrainian capital to flee out of the country. Virtually all international ratings and investment climate surveys place Ukraine among the least advanced transition economies.

More specific indicators of the problems accountable for the rather negative perception of Ukraine's investment climate are provided by a "Business Environment and Enterprise Performance Survey" carried out by the EBRD for its 1999 Transition Report. For the purposes of this survey, the managers of over 3 000 enterprises in twenty Central and East European and CIS countries were asked to assess the business/investment climate in their respective countries.

Questions focused on macroeconomic conditions (policy instability, inflation, exchange rate), microeconomic conditions (business regulations and taxation, and access to finance), law and order (functioning of the judiciary, corruption, crime) and physical infrastructure. Out of the 20 countries surveyed, Ukraine occupied the 16th place, ahead of Russia (17th place) and behind Kazakhstan and Georgia.[18] However, on microeconomic conditions alone, Ukraine scored lowest of all the 20 countries. Ukraine was also at to the bottom (ahead only of Moldova and behind Russia) with respect to its effectiveness in affording security of property and contract rights.[19]

In 1999, a German advisory group to the Ukrainian Government asked 20 companies operating in Ukraine to list the 20 most important impediments for investing in Ukraine and rank them in the order of their disincentive potential. Legal uncertainty was rated as the first and foremost impediment by all companies interviewed, placing Ukraine in this respect considerably behind Russia. Further disincentives emanating from the public policy area related to Government's failure to abide by its commitments (rank 3), Government control and remnants of command economy (rank 4), lack of support from authorities (rank 6), corruption (rank 7) and long processes for obtaining necessary permits (rank 8).[20]

The foregoing observations are supported by the findings of a "Report on Impediments to Foreign Investment in Ukraine" carried out by the TACIS-funded Ukrainian-European Policy and Legal Advice Centre in 1999. This report was based on interviews with some 22 leading law offices, accounting and business consulting firms in Ukraine. It concludes that substantive flaws in Ukraine's legislation are secondary to an overall climate of the lack of transparency and insecurity characterised by arbitrary application of continuously altering legislation with often retroactive force.[21]

A 1999 diagnostic study carried out on behalf of the United States Agency for International Development (USAID) compared the reform progress in seven key areas of commercial law in four countries: Poland, Romania, Ukraine and Kazakhstan. The seven areas are bankruptcy, collateral, company, competition, contract, foreign direct investment and trade legislation. Although the study used a new methodology that has since been modified, it is noteworthy that Ukraine scored lowest overall. Nonetheless in some areas of legislation (such as the law on pledges) considerable progress was acknowledged.

A June 2000 survey conducted by the International Centre for Policy Studies[22] on Foreign Direct Investment in Ukraine ranked the major deterrents to FDI in Ukraine in the following order (descending in significance):

- unstable and excessive regulations;
- ambiguity of the legal system;
- uncertainty of the economic environment;
- corruption;
- high tax burden;
- problems establishing clear ownership conditions;
- depressed disposable income levels;
- difficulty negotiating with government and privatisation authorities;
- volatility of the political environment;
- lack of physical infrastructure; and
- problems in entering domestic and export markets.

The policy agenda priorities suggested by the survey respondents comprised the liberalisation of capital, foreign exchange and profit expatriation controls, the lifting of restrictions on foreign ownership and control, the minimisation of red tape, and the reduction of tax rates and number of taxes.

3. Foreign Investment Regime

3.1. Investment Protection

3.1.1. Foreign Investment Law

The legal regime specifically addressing foreign investments is set out in both domestic legislation and international treaties of Ukraine. The "Law on the Regime of Foreign Investment" of March 1996 (the Foreign Investment Law) provides the principal rules for the treatment of foreign investments in Ukraine. More specifically, the Law:

- in principle permits both partial and total foreign ownership of Ukrainian enterprises (Article 3);
- in principle assures foreign investments and enterprises with foreign investments "national treatment", i.e., treatment at least as favourable as that accorded to domestic Ukrainian enterprises [Article7 (1)];
- guarantees the free conversion and transfer of profits from and other payments in relation to foreign investments in Ukraine (Article 12);
- provides guarantees against nationalisation and expropriation (Article 9, 10);
- ensures foreign investors compensation of any losses, resulting from unlawful action or inaction of state bodies or government officials (Article 10);
- shields investments against subsequent changes of legislation with respect to any of the above-mentioned guarantees for a ten year period, so-called "Stabilisation Clause" (Article 8); and
- exempts from customs duties capital goods, which are imported into Ukraine and accounted for as assets of an enterprise with foreign investment (Article 18).

While these guarantees at first glance appear to meet international standards, some caveats must be added. To begin with, the Foreign Investment Law in its 26 articles contains a total of 27 provisos in favour of domestic legislation; notably the national treatment principle is qualified by such a proviso. These provisos are normally open-ended so that only a review of all Ukrainian legislation applicable to a foreign investment operation provides legal certainty.

Furthermore, the above-mentioned guarantees against expropriation and illegal actions of state bodies apply only to the rights of foreign investors as owners of or shareholders in enterprises with foreign investments. They do not extend to the rights and assets of such enterprises themselves. Investors are hence not protected under the Foreign Investment Law against state interference in the operations of enterprises with foreign investments and a resultant dilution of the economic value of their investments.

The Foreign Investment Law also provides recourse to domestic Ukrainian courts only; international arbitration is only available where established in an applicable international treaty of Ukraine (Article 26).

3.1.2. International Commercial Arbitration

Contracts between Ukraine and foreign parties may provide for international commercial arbitration, either in Ukraine or abroad (Law on International Arbitration of April 1994 in conjunction with Law on Foreign Economic Activity of April 1991). In Ukraine, two permanent arbitration fora have been established, both at the Chamber of Commerce and Industry – the International Commercial Arbitration Court and the Maritime Arbitration Commission. While the Arbitration Law establishes the exclusivity of arbitral proceedings (if validly agreed) and Ukraine has joined the 1958 UN Convention on the Recognition and Enforcement of Foreign Arbitral Awards (New York Convention), uncertainties remain with respect to the enforcement of arbitral awards. A new law is presently being prepared to ensure effective enforcement of arbitral awards.

3.1.3. Investment Protection Treaties

The above-mentioned shortcomings of the foreign investment legislation should, however, not be overstated. Ukraine has concluded some 67 bilateral investment protection treaties ("BITs"),[23] 43 of which are in force. The treaty network includes the major source countries of foreign investments in Ukraine, such as the United States, Germany, the Netherlands, Russia, France, the United Kingdom, Belgium and Canada.

Ukraine has furthermore signed several multilateral agreements related to foreign investments, most notably the Washington Convention on Settlement of International Disputes between States and Individuals of 1965 (the so-called ICSID Convention), the Partnership and Co-operation Agreement of 1998 with the European Union and the 1994 Energy Charter Treaty which in its section 3 provides a comprehensive regime for the protection of investments in the energy sector.

Under the Ukrainian Constitution (Article 9), international treaties are *ipso jure* integral parts of the Ukrainian legal system and directly applicable. They supersede the Foreign Investment Law and prevail over it in case of conflict (Article 6 of the Foreign Investment Law).

The bilateral investment protection treaties of Ukraine in most cases conform to international standards. They in particular provide comprehensive guarantees

---

Box 1. **Energy Charter Treaty**

The 1994 Energy Charter Treaty (ECT), which provides a legally-binding foundation for inter-governmental co-operation in the area of energy trade, transit, investments and energy efficiency, has been signed or acceded to by 51 states. Following the Ukrainian parliament's ratification of the ECT on 29 October 1998, the Treaty entered into force for Ukraine on 27 January 1999. In accordance with Article 10 of the ECT, its Contracting Parties are required to accord national treatment or most-favoured nation treatment, whichever is the more favourable, to investors of other Contracting Parties in the energy sector once their investment has been made.

For potential investors of other Contracting Parties looking to invest in the energy sector, the ECT obliges Contracting Parties "to endeavour to" accord this same standard of non-discriminatory treatment. Those Contracting Parties that maintain laws, regulations or other measures that constitute exceptions to this latter best-efforts commitment are obliged to notify them, and such exceptions are kept under regular review by the ECT's governing body, the Energy Charter Conference.

Ukraine maintains seven such exceptions.[24] Potentially the most significant of these relate to land ownership and to procedures for determining the share of state property offered for sale to foreign investors when privatising state enterprises. The Energy Charter Secretariat has requested clarification from the Ukrainian government concerning the application in practice of the national measures that it has notified as constituting exceptions to the ECT's investment provisions, and how they might be discriminatory in relation to foreign investors. Pending such clarification, it is expected that a more thorough analysis will be provided by an Energy Charter Review of Ukraine's non-conforming measures, which is tentatively scheduled for the spring of 2001.

Of relevance also to the general investment climate in Ukraine are the ECT's provisions on energy transit, in accordance with which Contracting Parties are obliged "to take the necessary measures to facilitate the transit of energy materials and products consistent with the principle of freedom of transit and without distinction as to ... origin, destination or ownership... or discrimination as to pricing on the basis of such distinctions, and without imposing any unreasonable delays, restrictions or charges" (Article 7(1) of ECT). The ECT transit-related provisions are soon to be supplemented by the adoption of a legally binding Energy Charter Transit Protocol, negotiations on which are currently under way.

Source: *Energy Charter Treaty Secretariat, Brussels.*

---

against nationalisation and expropriation (including guarantees against indirect and creeping expropriation) which extend to the assets of the enterprises with foreign investments. They usually guarantee national treatment without qualifying provisos. They also offer recourse to international arbitration for the resolution of any disputes between either the state parties to the treaty (state-to-state disputes) or protected foreign investors and Ukraine (investor-state disputes). More than 30 investment protection treaties include so-called ISCID clauses providing access to the investment dispute settlement centre affiliated with the World Bank as soon as the ICSID Convention enters into force with respect to Ukraine; it was ratified in March 2000.

All investment protection treaties reviewed furthermore ensure investors from the contracting states the best treatment that Ukraine has accorded to investors from any other country in an investment-related treaty (so-called most-favoured-nation-treatment). As a consequence, investors from countries with investment protection treaties with Ukraine can claim the best treatment that Ukraine has agreed to in a treaty with any third country. For instance, a Dutch investor can invoke provisions of the Ukrainian-German investment protection treaty and a German investor provisions of the treaty between Ukraine and the United States.

Guarantees contained in all investment protection treaties of Ukraine hence add up to a comprehensive protection framework available to all investors from all countries with which Ukraine has concluded such treaties. As these countries practically include all major capital-exporting countries, the shortcomings of the Foreign Investment Law are largely remedied by the existing treaty framework.

While domestic legislation can in principle be altered any time by subsequent legislation, international treaties can not be legally reneged before their expiry without the consent of the other state party. With the exception of the investment protection treaty with China, all investment protection treaties of Ukraine have terms between ten and twenty years. Guarantees contained in such treaties are hence for this period of time shielded against any changes in Ukrainian legislation. The treaties thus also supersede limitations of the above-mentioned stabilisation clause of the Ukrainian Foreign Investment Law.

3.2. Investment Liberalisation

While the overall legal framework is acceptable, the application and implementation leave much to be desired because of institutional and administrative impediments. Most investment protection treaties of Ukraine confine themselves to statements of political intent with respect to the admission of foreign investments ("pre-establishment treatment"). Only the investment protection treaty with the United States as well as the Partnership and Co-operation Agreement (PCA) with the European Union extend national treatment to the establishment of companies, thus entitling United States and European investors to assume business operations in Ukraine on the same conditions as domestic Ukrainian entrepreneurs.

47

However, even under these treaties, the right of establishment is subject to some sector-specific exceptions [see Article II (1) and annex of the Ukrainian – United States BIT and Article 30 para. 2 in conjunction with Annex 5 of the PCA]. It would require further legal analysis to determine whether the above-mentioned treaty provisions, via the principle of most favoured nation treatment, extend to investors from countries other than the United States and the European Union.

The above-mentioned Foreign Investment Law in principle permits foreign investments through participation in enterprises jointly with Ukrainian partners ("joint ventures"), the creation or acquisition of wholly-owned subsidiaries, and branch operations (Article 3 of the Foreign Investment Law). Under Article 4 of the same law, however, access of foreign investments to Ukraine is subject to a general proviso of domestic legislation.

Despite some liberalisation in recent years, limitations on foreign participation remain in certain sectors, notably insurance, banking, television, telecommunications and broadcasting. However, such restrictions can to some extent be overcome by an indirect participation via local subsidiaries.

A horizontal discrimination of foreign investors furthermore exists in the Land Code 1991/92 under which foreigners and enterprises with foreign investments are not allowed to acquire ownership of land even in cases where domestic Ukrainian enterprises are permitted to do so. A new draft Land Code has, however, been introduced to Parliament in spring 2000, which would largely remedy the situation.

Box 2.   **Discrimination of foreign investors in certain sectors**

Insurance

- Only insurance companies registered in Ukraine may carry out insurance operations.
- Minimum capital requirement is an equivalent of 100 000 Euro for domestic insurance companies, but 500 000 Euro equivalent for insurance companies with foreign shareholders.
- Foreign share in Ukrainian insurance companies is limited to 49 per cent of registered capital.

Television and Broadcasting

Foreign share in Ukrainian television and broadcasting companies is limited to 30 per cent of registered capital, and has to be permitted by the National Board of Television and Broadcasting.

Despite the remaining discrimination of foreign investors, the overall legal framework for foreign direct investment must be regarded as acceptable by international standards. Thus, Ukraine's legal framework for FDI was rated higher than that of Poland in the above-mentioned USAID report (89 per cent over 87 per cent). However, the overall legal, institutional and administrative framework for foreign investment was rated remarkably lower than that of Poland (41 per cent as compared to 77 per cent).

3.3. Incentives and Privileges

While initial foreign investment legislation offered considerable incentives to foreign investors, most were removed by subsequent legislation. The Foreign Investment Decree of 1993 in particular offered a five-year tax holiday on profits for enterprises with qualifying foreign investment. The 1996 Foreign Investment Law abolished this incentive but grandfathered it for enterprises registered before the end of 1994. With respect to these enterprises, the privilege was repealed by special legislation as of July 1997, *i.e.* before the expiry of the grandfathered tax holiday. Several enterprises challenged this allegedly retroactive repeal before the Constitutional Court. While the Constitutional Court had admitted this challenge for consideration, it dismissed it in October 1999 on procedural grounds without a decision on the merits.

The general trend against investment incentives notwithstanding, in September 1997 a law "On the Promotion of Automobile Production" and implementing Government Decrees provided a range of privileges for automobile manufacturers with at least $150 million foreign investment via bank transfer. They include exemption from import duties for automobile components and exemption of the sale of cars in Ukraine from value added tax until January 2008, as well as protection against competing used car imports by prohibiting entirely the import of cars older than eight years and imposing a fictitious minimum value of $5 000 on imported cars for customs purposes. This legislation was obviously intended to facilitate a joint venture between the ailing Ukrainian AvtoZAZ and the South Korean Daewoo Corporation. On the objections of the European Commission,[25] the protection against competing imports was relaxed in spring 2000.

On 17 February 2000, a new law was adopted for the stated purpose of eliminating discrimination of domestically-owned *vis-à-vis* foreign-owned enterprises in Ukraine. It introduces equal treatment of foreign and domestic enterprises with respect to taxation, customs and currency regulations. The sole exception is for preferences of foreign investors established by international treaties as well as the above-mentioned privileges of Daewoo/AvtoZAZ. By the same token, Presidential Decree No. 240/2000 of 15 February 2000 instructs the Government to review the expediency of remaining privileges to foreign investors.

3.4. Special Economic Zones

Since 1996, a total of 21[26] special economic zones (SEZ) or priority development areas (PDA) have been established, reportedly covering some 10 per cent of Ukrainian territory. The creation of free economic zones has been adopted as a method of regional industrial development. The general procedure for the creation of, and activity in, free economic zones is set out by the Law of Ukraine "On the General Conditions for the Creation and Operation of Special Economic Zones" of October 1992.

Each special economic zone is created and operated within a framework provided by a special law. Incentives in terms of taxation, customs regime, finance and other aspects are offered to foreign and domestic investors in these areas. Further privileges are granted to high-priority enterprises in such zones as well as to export-oriented and import substitution manufacturers. Usually, benefits include tax holidays (five years for profit tax, three years for land tax and 50 per cent discounts thereafter), as well as exceptions from import and excise duties and import VAT.

Admission into an SEZ is frequently limited to large investors (e.g., investors investing more than $1 million in the SEZ). Enterprises within SEZs are subject to strict regulation and supervision by both the local bodies and the central Agency on Special Economic Zones. The latter was created in May 1999 but integrated into the Ministry of Economy in early 2000. Procedures on the admission of investors to and their exiting from SEZs as well as the powers of bodies entitled to interfere with business activities in SEZs remain opaque.[27]

According to official statistics, 21 zones have attracted some 260 investment projects worth $1.3 billion over the past two years. Performance of the various zones differs considerably, though, and only 3 of the 21 zones are considered as successes, notably the Donetsk zone, which alone attracted some $237 million dollars. Most of these, however, ended up in Donetsk city rather than the neighbouring depressed coal-mining villages as hoped. The share of foreign investments in projects in SEZs remains modest, and there are indications that existing business activities are moved into the zones just to benefit from the incentives.

To a significant extent, investments in these zones seem to come at the expense of investments elsewhere in the country. While the costs of the zones (some 350 million hrvyna in lost tax revenue in 2000 alone and more expected in subsequent years) are real, the zones' success in mobilising additional investments (i.e. investments that would not have been made anyway in Ukraine) remains subject to question. Furthermore, the fiscal benefits granted to business within the zones distort competition with business outside them.

For these reasons, the present system of SEZs and PDAs is widely criticised, including by the IMF and the EU. In view of this criticism, a moratorium was announced on creating new zones until 2003 in the Law on the Budget for 2000.

3.5. Laws on Production-Sharing and on Concession Agreements

In fall 1999, legislation intended to attract private investments into mineral resources and public infrastructure projects entered into force – the Law "On Production-sharing Agreements" and the Law "On Concession Agreements". The former deals with the exploration and exploitation of mineral resources and the latter with the construction and operation of infrastructure projects (transportation, energy, and water supply).

This legislation differs in two respects from similar legislation in other transition countries: i) The concept of production-sharing agreements is extended to all mineral resources projects (and not confined only to oil and gas); and ii) concession agreements are envisaged only for infrastructure projects (not for mining projects). While the two laws apply to domestic and foreign investors alike, in practice they address primarily potential foreign investors.

The legislation establishes strict requirements on the one hand, especially with respect to production-sharing agreements, including local content and local employment requirements – to the detriment of flexibility. On the other hand, the legislation includes exemptions from mandatory legislation for contractors, notably:

- an exemption from export proceeds surrender requirements,
- an exemption from import licensing requirements for equipment needed to implement the project, and
- freezing of applicable domestic legislation as of the time of the conclusion of the agreement.

Each production-sharing agreement will have to be approved by an interdepartmental commission to be created in the Cabinet of Ministers and composed of Government, Parliament and local government representatives.

The new legislation will have to be tested in practice. Thus far, no actual production-sharing or concession agreement has been reported, although some negotiations are apparently pending. Perhaps, both mandatory requirements and administrative procedures will have to be relaxed to facilitate deals.

3.6. Institutional/Administrative Framework

While some countries have established particular institutions with primary responsibility for promoting foreign direct investment (e.g. the Polish State Agency of Foreign Investment), in Ukraine responsibility for FDI related activities is dispersed among several institutions at the central, provincial and local levels. At the central level, these institutions included, until the end of 1999, the National Agency for Development and European Integration (NADEI), the Ministry of Economy, the Ministry of Foreign Economic Relations, the State Committee on Investment and Clearing, the State Investment Corporation (Derzhinvest) and the Agency for Special Economic Zones. Within the context of privatisation, foreign investment matters are handled by the State Property Fund. Foreign investments as such are required to be registered with the regional state administrations where the investment would be located.

Within the framework of a major restructuring of the Ukrainian Government through Presidential Decree of December 1999, the NADEI, the Ministry of Foreign Economic Relations, the State Investment and Clearing Committee and the Agency for Special Economic Zones have all been integrated into the Ministry of Economy; Derzhinvest was liquidated.

The dispersal of responsibilities without clear demarcation lines had embroiled the various ministries/agencies in turf battles and forestalled the development and implementation of a coherent investment promotion strategy. While foreign investors receive support from some of the above-mentioned agencies in individual cases, there is no single institution that could provide support consistently and effectively. Accordingly, while the legal framework for FDI in Ukraine has received high marks, the implementing FDI institutions have been rated poorly; in the above-mentioned USAID report they reached 18 per cent as compared with 82 per cent in Poland and 58 per cent in Romania.

For several years, the creation of a central investment promotion agency has been considered, but failed mainly due to jurisdictional controversies among interested government institutions. In the meantime, investment promotion agencies or companies have been established in many regions, such as the Kiev Investment Agency and the Odessa Bureau for Foreign Investments. The success of these regional initiatives seems to be mixed at best. They appear to be more constrained by the agencies' managerial capacities than a lack of interested investors.

3.6.1. *Foreign Investment Advisory Council*

In April 1997, a Foreign Investment Advisory Council was established by Presidential Decree as a forum for an ongoing policy dialogue between the senior Ukrainian economic policy-makers and foreign company executives. The Council is chaired by the President of Ukraine and comprises, on the Ukrainian side, the Prime Minister, the Minister of Economy and the Chairman of the National Bank. On the international side, the Council consists of some 23 chief executive officers of major multinational enterprises with investments in Ukraine, plus the EBRD representative.

Thus far, the Council met three times. While it had some results (for instance, the suspension of the so-called *kartoteka* system, its role could be strengthened by a permanent working body ensuring appropriate follow-up on the conclusions of Council meetings. Such a body could bring together experts from both sides. Some representatives of business associations to address the particular interests and problems of small and medium-sized enterprises could also be included. The proposed OECD-Ukraine Forum on Investment and Enterprise Development could develop synergies with the Council for achieving common objectives.

3.6.2. *Chamber of Independent Experts on Foreign Investment Issues*

In 1997 the President has also formed a Chamber of Independent Experts, designed to serve as a non-binding arbitration forum for dispute cases between foreign investors and Ukrainian authorities.[28] The Chamber includes 14 members (all lawyers), 7 of whom are foreign nationals. For concrete proceedings, panels of (normally 3) chamber members are constituted. While the conclusions of the panels are not binding on the parties, they are directly submitted to the President of Ukraine for a final decision.

Thus far, the Chamber has considered some 10 cases and in most cases its decisions were voluntarily followed by the parties, including Ukrainian authorities. For instance, an advisory opinion of the Chamber on the application of the value added tax to foreign investments had contributed to an amendment of the VAT Law.

Despite weaknesses, especially with respect to implementing institutions, Ukraine's foreign investment regime cannot be held accountable for the overall poor rating of Ukraine's investment climate. As foreign investors operate in Ukraine alongside with domestic enterprises, they are also affected by the general legal framework and administrative practices applying to domestic and foreign enterprises alike. It is the flaws in this general framework which provide the main disincentives to foreign and domestic entrepreneurial activity in Ukraine and thus explain the parallel between low foreign investment (and in fact negative investment flows if capital flight is taken into account) and negative economic growth.

4. Rule of Law: From Piecemeal Legislation to an Effective Legal System

4.1. Much Legislation, Little System

There is no lack of legislation in Ukraine. On the contrary, investors complain of the abundance of the often inconsistent and conflicting legislation. When it gained independence, Ukraine inherited a vast body of Soviet law. This is still in force today to the extent that it has not been expressly repealed or superseded by post-independence legislation. The inconsistent and unclear regime gives rise to unpredictable administration and interpretation, which in turn invites corrupt practices and behaviour, both in the civil service and elsewhere.

In terms of sheer numbers, legislative activities since independence look impressive. Almost 2000 new laws were enacted; together all primary and secondary legislation (presidential decrees, government and central bank regulations) reportedly account for some 30 000 so-called "normative acts" (implementing regulations). While this avalanche of legislation has introduced noticeable reforms in some areas (such as privatisation, price and trade liberalisation), it has hitherto achieved little progress in terms of legal certainty and stability as well administrative efficiency, transparency and integrity.

This is mainly due to the fact that legislation is normally adopted piece-meal to introduce specific policy measures in response to the day-to-day needs and political pressures. It does not reflect a systematic process designed to enact a coherent reform strategy based on a comprehensive rule of law concept and a long-term policy vision for Ukraine. Thus far, reform legislation has failed to create a coherent interdependent system where legal acts in various domains build on one another and supplement each other. Gaps and inconsistencies between pieces of legislation remain frequent.

The problem is compounded by a tendency of Ukrainian legislation – inherited from the Soviet past – to confine laws to restatements of general principles to be specified in secondary legislation and administrative instructions. As a result, laws frequently become meaningful only in conjunction with several pieces of secondary legislation (which often are not easily accessible) – to the detriment of transparency. There is also a considerable body of incomplete legislation – laws that are not yet applicable in practice because implementing regulations, resolutions and/or instructions are still outstanding.

Inconsistency furthermore emanates from the fact that four institutions independently of each other have the right of legislative initiative: the Government (Cabinet of Ministers), the President, the members of the Parliament and the National Bank. Among these institutions, and in the past most notably between Government and Parliament, there is little co-ordination. As a result, draft bills on related topics may be prepared in parallel in the Government and Parliament, which might be inspired by different concepts. The drafts are then usually compared in the Parliamentary Committee preparing drafts for the readings in the Plenary. However, there is no procedure ensuring an examination of draft bills for their systemic consistency. If drafts end up in different committees (which can easily happen in case of sector legislation), they might not be compared at all.

The systemic deficiencies of Ukrainian law almost preclude its consistent and predictable application in practice. The problem is aggravated by weaknesses of Ukrainian law enforcement institutions and its civil service.

What is urgently needed therefore is a change from piece-meal legislation to a step-by-step process towards a coherent legal system, starting with fundamental legislation that provides the basic concepts on which the system can be built. The beginning has been made in June 1996 with the adoption of the Constitution of Ukraine.

4.2. 1996 Constitution

The 1996 Constitution lays a solid ground for shaping a market-economy legal system in Ukraine under the rule of law. It

- commits Ukraine to the principles of democracy, rule of law and social welfare (Article 1);
- divides state powers among legislative, executive and judicial branches (Article 6);
- recognises private ownership, including private ownership of land (articles 13,14);
- guarantees free disposition of property and submits any expropriation to a procedure prescribed by law and providing for "previous and full compensation" (Article 41);
- ensures entrepreneurial freedom and the protection of competition in business (Article 42);
- guarantees foreign residents in Ukraine, including foreign investors, the same rights and freedoms as Ukrainian citizens, albeit under the proviso of Ukrainian laws and international treaties (Article 26);
- guarantees compensation for losses from illegal action or inaction of public authorities or officials (Article 56);
- requires publication of all legislation as a condition of its validity (Article 57);
- outlaws retroactive legislation (Article 58);

- provides recourse to courts against acts of public authorities and officials (Article 55); and

- requires the creation of an independent judiciary with specialised courts by June 2001 (articles 124 ff and Chapter XV, para. 12).

To guarantee the implementation of the Constitution, a Constitutional Court was established in October 1996. Under the Law "On the Constitutional Court" of October 1996, individuals and companies may request an authoritative interpretation of any provision of the Constitution and any law of Ukraine. However, such requests must be accepted by the Constitutional Court at its free discretion. Amendments providing for a right of individuals to appeal to the Constitutional Court are under consideration.

While the Constitution marks a promising beginning for building a consistent and integrated legal system, other fundamental codifications are awaiting adoption or are still in the drafting process.

4.3. Civil Code

In continental European market economies, civil codes are at the core of contract and property protection. In Ukraine, the Soviet civil code of 1963 is still in force, though it was amended since independence more than a hundred times. A new comprehensive draft Civil Code had been adopted by Parliament in the first reading in June 1997, but since then parliamentary proceedings practically came to a halt until spring 2000. In May 2000, the draft – as amended in the light of comments received – has been adopted in its second reading.

The draft has been inspired by Western European civil codes, notably the German "Bürgerliches Gesetzbuch" and the Dutch Civil Code of 1992. It also takes into account the CIS Model Civil Code and the modern civil codes adopted in the 1990s in Russia and other CIS countries.

The draft Code encompasses the subject matters usually addressed in Western civil codes, namely a general part providing basic definitions and concepts, which apply to the entire code; property rights; obligations; family law; and inheritance law. In addition to this classic content of civil codes, the draft covers 1) personal non-property rights of individuals, 2) intellectual property protection and 3) private international law (conflict of laws).

The function of the draft Civil Code is the same as in continental European market economies, namely to provide the basic concepts and terminology for the entire private law system[29] – thus ensuring its coherence. Legislation in such areas as company law, secured lending, consumer protection and rules of civil procedure are supposed to build on the civil code and implement its principles.

It is for these reasons that most CIS countries, in shaping their market economy legal systems, have given priority to adopting modern civil codes.

Ukraine, Moldova and Tajikistan are the only CIS countries which have failed to do so thus far. A modern civil code of Ukraine would be a milestone in remedying the present conceptual and terminological opaqueness of Ukrainian law.

4.4. Judiciary System

The present court system comprises the Constitutional Court, the "courts of general jurisdiction" and *arbitrazh* courts. The latter are in charge of commercial disputes arising between enterprises, other organisations and individual entrepreneurs with respect to "commercial contracts" as well as of bankruptcy cases and antimonopoly cases. The *arbitrazh* courts were created in 1991 by transforming the state *arbitrazh* system, which was in charge of economic disputes in Soviet times between state entities, into courts. General courts are organised at three levels – municipal first instances, 27 courts of appeal (one in each *oblast*), and the Supreme Court in Kiev; the *arbitrazh* courts, on the other hand, operate only at two levels – 27 first instances in the *oblasts* and the Supreme Arbitrazh Court in Kiev as the only appeals instance.

Previously, court protection against illegal action or inaction of public authorities practically did not exist. In 1996 the rules of procedure of the courts of general jurisdiction and the *arbitrazh* courts were amended to authorise the courts to annul illegal acts of public authorities and award compensation for damages resulting from unlawful acts of public officials.

As a consequence, appeals by economic agents against acts of public authorities to the *arbitrazh* courts have been mushrooming, reaching some 20 500 cases in 1999. Most of those concerned tax issues. Even though these statistics reflect progress in judicial protection against misuse of power, shortcomings remain. Unlike in some Western systems, appeals against administrative acts do not suspend the effect of such acts until a court decision is taken.

Improvements are reportedly still needed in the preliminary legal protection before formal institution of court proceedings, both with respect to the enforcement of contract and property rights and the protection against illegal action or inaction by public authorities. As regards the defence of contract and property rights, effective preliminary protection is especially important in view of the so-called "pretensiya" system requiring the creditor to give the debtor a one-month advance notice before filing suit (the "pretensiya" does not apply to suits against acts of public authorities).

Until recently, the enforcement of awards involved lengthy procedures with uncertain results. Reportedly, about one-third of court awards were not executed. In 1998 new legislation on the enforcement of awards was adopted and the implementing system was placed under the supervision of the Ministry of Justice. Appropriately notarised deeds are in some cases directly enforceable.

57

Under the Constitution (Article 125 and chapter XV, para. 12), a new court system must be created by June 2001. The new system would establish the jurisdiction of the Supreme Court over all types of disputes and ensure an adequate specialisation of courts or chambers within courts.

A draft law on reorganising the judiciary system had been adopted in Parliament in the first reading in late 1999. In the wake of the Parliamentary reshuffle in spring 2000, however, this draft lost the support of the majority and a competing draft was presented by the new chair of the legal policy committee.

Under both drafts, at least three branches of courts are envisaged – courts of general jurisdiction (although it remains disputed whether these would handle both civil and criminal cases or whether separate civil and criminal courts should be created), economic courts for commercial disputes (absorbing the present *arbitrazh* courts) and administrative courts for suits against public authorities. Under both drafts also, all branches would have a first instance, an appeals instance and a "cour de cassation". No agreement has, however, been reached on three questions namely:

- the question whether the Supreme Court becomes the "cour de cassation" for all three branches or whether each branch will have a supreme court of its own;

- the question whether the presidents of the courts at all levels will be appointed by the President of Ukraine at the recommendation of the Ministry of Justice (except the President(s) of the Supreme Court(s) who would be elected by the members of that court(s) on nomination of the President), or whether they will be elected by the judges of the courts concerned; and

- the question whether the budget of the court system will be controlled by the Ministry of Justice or by the self-regulatory bodies of the judiciary.

It is envisaged that within three months of the adoption of the new law on the court system, new rules of civil procedure and an entirely new code of administrative court procedure are to be adopted. Drafts are presently finalised. Discussion is still pending on the question whether separate rules of procedure are needed for economic courts or whether these will operate under the same rules of civil procedure as the courts of general jurisdiction.

4.5. Approximation to European Standards

In June 1998, the presidential decree set out a "Strategy of Ukraine's Integration into the European Union". This strategy provides for the approximation of Ukrainian law to that of the European Union. The decree was followed up by an August 1999 Cabinet of Ministers resolution elaborating on the concept of approximation.

Under this resolution, approximation shall proceed in a gradually planned process including three stages. During the first (present) stage, priority will be given to bringing Ukrainian legislation into compliance with Ukraine's commitments under the Partnership and Co-operation Agreement (PCA) and on building the legal fundamentals for a functioning market economy under the rule of law. Approximation shall also proceed in key areas, notably legislation on entrepreneurship, competition, bankruptcy, intellectual property protection, customs regulations, transport and communications, as well as technical standards and certification.

During the second stage, approximation shall extend to further areas of economic law prioritised in the PCA, such as company law, banking law, environment protection (see article 51 para. 2 of the PCA); and the legal requirements shall be fulfilled for a free trade area between Ukraine and the European Union.

The third and final stage is conditional on the conclusion of the Association Agreement between Ukraine and the European Union. It envisages a comprehensive programme transforming the entire body of EC legislation (the so-called "acquis communautaire") into Ukrainian legislation with a view to preparing Ukraine for eventual EU membership.

5. Company Law

5.1. Present Legislation

Two laws adopted right after Ukraine gained independence (so-called first generation legislation) provide the legal underpinning for business enterprises in Ukraine, namely the Law on Enterprises of March 1991 and the Law of Companies of September 1991. Business enterprises can be created alternatively under either law, but the provisions of the Law on Enterprises in any case extend to companies established under the Company Law. The Enterprise Law offers six types of enterprise organisations, a company being one of them. The Company Law furthermore provides a choice among five different types of companies (joint-stock companies, limited liability companies, additional liability companies, general partnerships and limited liability partnerships).

Despite this range of options, foreign ventures in Ukraine in practice are established in one of the four alternative forms below:

i) a representative office (which is not a legal entity);

ii) a wholly owned foreign subsidiary (usually in the form of limited liability company);

iii) a joint venture (either in the form of a joint stock company or a limited liability company); or

iv) an agreement on joint co-operation and production, which does not require registration of a separate legal entity.[30]

Subsidiaries and joint ventures are considered as Ukrainian corporate entities and thus as residents of Ukraine for tax and currency regulation purposes; representative offices, on the other hand, are not considered as residents.

The Enterprise Law includes comprehensive requirements for the social protection of employees and self-governance rights of trade unions. These provisions also extend to companies established under the Company Law.

The enterprise/company legislation contains major weaknesses, especially with respect to:

- *Shareholder protection*

  Fiduciary duties that in most legal systems engage the responsibility of directors towards the company are totally lacking. The responsibility of general managers/directors to shareholders is limited to gross negligence. There are no provisions against asset stripping, share dilution, profit skimming and insider dealing. These problems are especially aggravated for minority shareholders and in cases where foreign participation is limited by law.[31]

- *Corporate finance*

  Different shares of stock are unknown, as are treasury shares that could facilitate capital increases. The total value of preferred stock is limited to 10 per cent and that of bonds to 25 per cent of an issuer's charter fund; interests on bonds may only be paid from net profit. Open joint stock companies may issue new shares only through public offerings and not through private placements. Payment on shares in joint stock and limited liability companies may not be made from borrowed funds.

- *Company register*

  A company register similar to those in Western market economies does not exist. The closest equivalent to such a register is a "Centralised Unified State Register of Enterprises and Companies in Ukraine" maintained by the State Committee on Statistics. This register represents a centralised computer database listing all business entities throughout Ukraine. Information is, however, limited to the following details: company name, identification code, name of director(s), address, fax and telephone numbers. The register in particular does not clarify the scope of company representatives' powers to act on behalf of the company; neither is reliance on information provided in the register legally protected.

• *State enterprises*

While the Enterprise Law also addresses state-owned enterprises, it fails to clarify creditor rights in case of such enterprises' default.

Box 3. **Misuse of Management Powers and Draft Law on Joint Stock Companies**

In the last several years, multiple events have taken place in the market that have clearly harmed investors' interests and were well publicised. The fallout from these events gave rise to discussions about the need for a new law on joint stock companies (JSC law). Perhaps most notoriously, the managers of the tyre manufacturer Dniproshina decided to issue shares at far below market value to insiders (share dilution).

In other companies, managers have moved substantial assets out of their companies without the company receiving a fair price for the property and without the approval of shareholders (asset stripping). Managers at still other companies have found creative ways to divert some of their company's profits to themselves, often through hidden side-agreements with suppliers or customers (profit skimming). The amazing thing is that current company law allows all of these practices.

The existing company law contains just 26 articles on joint stock companies, with many aspects of companies simply not regulated. A comprehensive JSC law, which protects shareholders' and creditors' rights, is critical for Ukraine. It will vastly improve the investment climate in the country. Ukrainian and foreign investors will have greater confidence in investing in Ukrainian companies, and shares of those companies will trade at higher values in the securities market. Ukrainian companies will thus be able to raise capital from investors more easily. And investors will be more willing to buy Ukrainian companies in the Government's privatisation programme, increasing the revenues to the Government from these sales.

Adoption of a strong JSC law is also a prerequisite for banking and financial sector development. First of all, banks themselves are joint stock companies. They will operate more effectively with a comprehensive and sound JSC law in place. Perhaps more importantly, the draft JSC should increase commercial lending to enterprises because it provides protections for creditors: *e.g.*,

---

61

Box 3.   **Misuse of Management Powers and Draft Law on Joint Stock Companies (*cont.*)**

limitations on payment of dividends, or purchase of its own shares in the secondary market, by an insolvent company as well as protections against profit skimming and asset stripping.

Against this background, a draft law on joint stock companies was prepared over the past two years under the auspices of the State Commission for Securities and Stock Markets and with the support of USAID. The draft takes into account the draft CIS model law on joint stock companies and the OECD "General Principles of Company Law in Transition Economies".

To the extent possible, the draft JSC law addresses actions by direct participants in the joint stock company (shareholders, the supervisory board, managers) rather than indirect participants (judges, regulators, legal and accounting professionals). Among other things, the draft law:

i) contains protections against share dilution, asset striping, profit skimming, and improper transactions with subsidiaries;

ii) defines more precisely the roles of the various bodies of a company;

iii) requires that large transactions be approved by the supervisory board or, above a certain ceiling, by the general shareholders meeting;

iv) limits dividends and acquisition by the company of its shares in order to protect the interests of creditors when a company is insolvent;

v) provides for appraisal and redemption rights for shareholders that vote against a reorganisation, major transaction or charter amendment limiting their rights;

vi) provides for liability of managers and directors;

vii) prohibits issuance of shares at other than market value;

viii) defines and requires pre-emptive rights; and

ix) requires cumulative voting so that minority shareholders are represented on supervisory boards.

The draft JSC law is expected to be submitted by the Cabinet of Ministers to the Rada shortly. Before proceeding with the draft, a decision should be taken on whether separate laws should be developed for the various types of business associations or whether all types should be covered by one comprehensive codification.

6. Taxation

There is a general problem in the application of tax laws and regulations because a hierarchy of tax rulings and interpretation is not necessarily recognised, causing conflicts between local and central officials.

Taxation tops the list of investment barriers in Ukraine. In the 1999 International Finance Corporation (IFC) Survey nearly all enterprises surveyed reported tax rates as a major problem; almost 90 per cent complained about the large number of taxes; and some 80 per cent expressed frustration about frequent changes of, and complexity in, tax legislation and reporting requirements. Unwillingness to comply with tax legislation drives an increasing number of companies into the shadow economy; according to the IFC, about half of the enterprises surveyed in 1998 hid up to 50 per cent of their profits from the tax authorities.[32]

6.1. The Tax System

In 1997 the Ukrainian Government submitted to Parliament eight draft laws intended to launch a comprehensive reform of the tax system. Of these, three were enacted, namely amendments to the Law "On the System of Taxation" (the Tax System Law), the Law "On Taxation of Profits of Enterprises" (the Corporate Tax Law) and the Law "On Value Added Tax" (the VAT Law). Under the Tax System Law there exist now 22 different central taxes and 16 types of local taxes (e.g. advertisement, parking, dog-owners). six of the 38 types of taxes generate more than 80 per cent of state revenues. These are:

 i) value added tax and import VAT (20 per cent);

 ii) corporate profit tax (rate: 30 per cent);

 iii) personal income tax (progressive up to 40 per cent);

 iv) social security contributions (37,5 per cent of the payroll);

 v) excise taxes (up to 300 per cent); and

 vi) import-export duties.

At 30 per cent, the corporate profit tax rate is one of the lowest in Europe (by comparison, the French and German regular rates are 45 per cent, Poland 32 per cent, Netherlands and Russia, 35 per cent) even though reductions of the rate are also pending in some countries (e.g. Poland, Russia, Germany). The actual tax burden is nevertheless exceptionally high due to unusual restrictions on amortisation and depreciation allowances. For instance, only "acquired" assets may be amortised but not assets "contributed" by shareholders to the charter fund of a subsidiary. The write-off of investments in a company's production facilities is also strictly limited. Corporate profits distributed as dividends are taxed as corporate profits (30 per cent) and secondly as income of shareholders (at a fixed 30 per cent rate); however, the shareholders' tax can be credited against that of the company so that in effect only one profit tax is levied. Dividends repatriated abroad are subject to a 15 per cent repatriation tax, which is in lieu of the 30 per cent tax for domestic shareholders but cannot be credited against the tax liabilities of the company. It might, however, be reduced or even eliminated through double taxation agreements.

Ukraine has concluded double taxation agreements with 40 countries as of 1 March 2001. These by and large conform to international standards; complaints of foreign investors in Ukraine abound, however, about failures on the part of Ukrainian tax authorities to apply these treaties properly.

The value added tax (VAT) is calculated on the difference between the VAT collected by a seller from its customers and the VAT paid to suppliers. At a standard rate of 20 per cent, it is in line with western market economies.

Like many Western economies, the Ukraine follows a self-assessment system, *i.e.* taxpayers must submit their own tax assessment to tax authorities and pay the tax according to their own calculations. However, because of withholding of wage income and an imputed income system for the smallest businesses, the vast majority of Ukrainian taxpayers are not obligated to compute their taxes and file tax returns.

Most of the problems could be avoided if there were more frequent and extensive consultations between tax authorities and tax payers, and especially accountants and auditors prior to enacting tax laws and regulations.

6.2. Problem Areas

Because of the self-assessment system, corporate taxpayers bear the risk of erroneous interpretation of tax legislation and wrong calculations. While this might be appropriate in clear and transparent tax environments, the ambiguities of and inconsistencies in the Ukrainian tax legislation give rise to serious interpretation problems, frequently leading to costly disputes between taxpayers and tax authorities.

The problem is aggravated by the imposition of high and sometimes exorbitant fines. These are frequently not related to the actual loss to the budget or the gravity of the tax payer's violation, but computed as standard fines corresponding to the equivalent of monthly salaries of the tax payer's general manager or chief accountant. Fines for late payments are also disproportionately high since they are calculated on a *per diem* basis.[33]

Further problems result from:

- the requirements that corporate taxpayers file quarterly declarations and make monthly payments on the basis of the actual taxable income earned in the previous month. Such requirements create enormous paperwork and are difficult to comply with;

- inconsistencies of many definitions used in the tax legislation with financial accounting principles and international practice; and

- the high level of payroll taxes, increasing labour costs by almost 40 per cent and forcing many companies into the "shadow" economy.

6.3. Improvements

While still deficient, remarkable improvements made in the Ukrainian tax system over the past few years should be recognised. Until mid 1999, local tax authorities were entitled to retain 30 per cent of the fines collected. This privilege induced them to impose maximum fines wherever possible and in many cases to resort to arbitrary interpretation of tax legislation in order to generate fines. Through the Parliamentary Resolution of July 1999 this privilege was abolished and tax authorities obligated to pay over all moneys collected to the state budget.

Until spring 1999, tax authorities had just withdrawn from taxpayers' bank accounts any amounts which in their opinion were owed by the taxpayer, without any notice or opportunity of prior judicial review (so-called *kartoteka*). In consonance with advice received at the Foreign Investor Advisory Council meeting in May 1999, this system is no longer applied in practice and taxpayers are notified of any impending enforcement of tax liabilities so that they are now able to seek court protection against enforcement actions.

It should further be acknowledged that the 1997 Corporate Tax Law broadened deductible business expenses, albeit not yet entirely in line with international practice.

The growing network of double taxation agreements moreover reflects Ukraine's efforts to bring its tax system into line with international standards.

In June 2000 the government submitted a comprehensive draft Tax Code to Parliament. If enacted, the Code would:

- decrease the VAT in two steps from 20 to 15 per cent;

- lower personal income tax rates from the present range of 10-40 per cent to 10-20 per cent;

- reduce the corporate profit tax in two steps from 30 to 20 per cent;

- introduce a property tax at a rate between 0.5 and 1 per cent;

- decrease the number of central taxes from 22 to 13 or 14 and the number of local taxes from 16 to 10; and

- provide simplified taxation procedures for small and medium-sized enterprises.

The Government hopes that the new tax system, by cutting the tax burden and easing compliance, will lessen the attractions of the shadow economy. Budget revenues are expected to drop by about 10 per cent after introduction of the new system, but the Government is counting on increasing the number of taxpayers by reducing the shadow economy. Independent experts, however, estimate that the envisaged reforms might result in higher than expected fiscal losses and that the tax base might not broaden as quickly as hoped for.

7. Property Protection and Secured Lending

Adequate recognition and protection of ownership rights is key to any market economy. Where the acquisition of ownership provides the basic incentive for investment, the use of ownership rights as collateral facilitates enterprise financing, and the ease of transfer of property determines the liquidity of markets.

7.1. Ownership System

In Ukraine, the basic rules on the scope, protection and transfer of property rights are still found in so-called "first generation legislation", namely the Law "On Ownership" of February 1991 and the Land Code of March 1992. When enacted shortly before Ukraine's declaration of independence, the Law on Ownership represented a milestone towards a market economy legal system. The Law recognises private ownership and enables foreigners to own property in Ukraine. It authorises property owners, including foreign investors, to use their property for commercial purposes, to lease property and retain the revenues and production derived from the use of property. However, the Ownership Law fails to establish a comprehensive regime for the protection, transfer and pledging of property.

7.1.1. Land-ownership

While the Ownership Law introduced remarkable, albeit incomplete, reforms towards market structures, the Land Code of March 1992 takes quite a restrictive view on land-ownership. Even though it recognises private land-ownership alongside state and collective, it declares state ownership as the principal form of land-ownership. The possibility to own land privately was granted to citizens of Ukraine only for the purposes of building private residencies and for agricultural subsistence. Corporations, Ukrainian and foreign, as well as foreign nationals are not allowed to own land.

Under the Land Code, corporations and foreigners may use land on the basis of land use or lease rights with lease rights in practice representing the only option for using land for industrial purposes. Such rights may be granted up to maximum of two forty-nine-year terms. While this time period normally captures the amortisation periods of investments, it provides insecurity as regards the stability of the terms of the lease and severely restricts the possibilities of transferring and mortgaging real estate.

Even though the 1992 Land Code is still in force, it is in part superseded by the Constitution of 1996. While the Land Code distinguishes between state, collective and private land-ownership, the Constitution in its Article 14 recognises state, municipal and private land-ownership, thus eliminating collective ownership as a category of its own and introducing municipal land-ownership in addition to state ownership. The Constitution also expressly recognises private land-ownership; however, it confirms the principle that the scope and exercise of land-ownership rights remain subject to limitations set forth in sub-constitutional legislation.

Several Presidential decrees furthermore introduced the possibility of acquiring land-ownership in special circumstances, such as the acquisition of incomplete construction sites. As these decrees are inconsistent with the Land Code, however, they are fraught with constitutional insecurity and have therefore failed to encourage real estate transactions on a substantial scale.

7.1.2. *Pending Reforms*

In April 2000, the Cabinet approved a new draft Land Code for submission to Parliament. The draft Code would legalise private ownership of land for both industrial and agricultural purposes; and it would allow foreigners to acquire non-arable land in urban areas for industrial purposes.

The draft Civil Code, if adopted, will provide the basic concepts of a market economy oriented ownership system, including the legal foundations of a mortgage system based on private land-ownership. Implementing legislation will, however, be required to make these concepts operative. Furthermore, the draft Civil Code refers to other, separate legislation all issues related to the administration of state property. While establishing every Ukrainian's right to own land, the draft still excludes foreigners from acquiring land. For foreign investors, however, this discrimination is softened by allowing all Ukrainian legal persons to own land, thus extending this right to wholly-owned foreign subsidiaries, even though still denying it to foreign companies operating branch offices in Ukraine.

7.2. Intellectual Property Protection

Under its Partnership and Co-operation Agreement with the EU, Ukraine has committed itself to bringing its system of intellectual property protection, by February 2003, to the level of that of the European Union (see Article 50 para. 1

and Annex III of the PCA). This commitment includes accession to a number of pertinent international agreements specified in Annex III of the PCA.

As of spring 2000, Ukraine is a party to the major agreements on the protection of international property, including the Convention Establishing the World Intellectual Property Organisation (WIPO), the Patent Co-operation Treaty of July 1970, the Madrid Agreement on Trade Marks of 1967, the Paris Convention for the Protection of Industrial Property of 1967 and the Geneva Gramophone Convention (1933) However, Ukraine is technically in violation of the provisions of the Paris Convention because foreign applicants must pay considerably higher fees for registering industrial property than domestic applicants (see Cabinet Decree "On State Fees" of January 1993).

As regards domestic legislation, the industrial property protection system is based on three laws which all entered into force in July 1994.[34] Until recently, the system was administered by the "Ukrainian State Patent Agency" ("Derzhpatent") which maintained a register of inventions, industrial designs and trade marks and issues patents on inventions and industrial designs. In summer 2000, *Derzhpatent* has been transformed into the "State Department for Intellectual Property", and it is still unclear which functions remain.

Domestic legislation and international treaties in theory provide a relatively comprehensive legal framework for industrial and intellectual property protection. Shortcomings remain, however, in the execution of the system. Fines for violations are insignificant and the powers of enforcement authorities weak. The enforcement system furthermore suffers from a lack of expertise in the *arbitrazh* courts, which are in charge of adjudicating industrial property violations.

As a result, complaints about industrial property violations abound. For instance, it is estimated that some 95 per cent of all computer software in use in Ukraine are pirated. To curb industrial property violations, a new law on the distribution of audio-visual products and gramophone recordings was adopted in March 2000, introducing control mechanisms over the distribution of these products.

7.3. Secured Lending

The possibilities of using property in Ukraine as collateral for loans differ considerably with respect to securities and real property.

7.3.1. *Pledging Securities*

Securities can be pledged under the Law "On Pledges" of October 1992. Until spring 1999, pledges remaining in the possession of debtors were, however, fraught with considerable insecurity, because the system relied on "books of pledge entries" maintained by the pledgers to provide notification of pre-existing pledges.

In March 1999, a state of the art "state securities pledge registry" was created and the Law "On Pledges" was amended to facilitate self-help seizure upon default. The registry, the first in its kind in any CIS country, is operated by "StateInfoJust" under the Ministry of Justice on a nation-wide scale through a central registry and 25 regional offices. Parties register pledges either directly with StateInfoJust or through a local bank or local notary. Tax authorities must furthermore register with the system any tax liabilities if they wish to have priority in the property of a delinquent taxpayer over subsequent pledge-holders.

As a consequence, the registry now establishes a reliable public mechanism to determine the priority order of pledges on pledged securities. It is envisaged to connect the system with the payments clearing system of the National Bank to which all banks of Ukraine are connected; this would give banks direct assess to the registry.[35]

7.3.2. Using Real Property as Collateral

In contrast to the relatively developed pledge system for securities, the possibilities of mortgage based lending remain underdeveloped. They are in practice confined to mortgages on private houses and apartments, documented in deeds prepared by notaries at the location of the real estate concerned. While notaries thus keep some documentation on titles to real estate in their district, there is no title registration system providing safeguards against pre-existing encumbrances and execution of mortgages remains fortuitous. Attempts at developing the mortgage system failed thus far due to controversy on the scope of private land-ownership. Unlike in Western market economies, the land under buildings remains in the ownership of the State or the municipality concerned even where the building is privately owned.

Two Presidential Decrees were issued in June 1999 to establish a mortgage system and a registry of titles to real estate. These decrees failed to enter into force due to parliamentary opposition. In spring 2000, the Government submitted to Parliament two interconnected draft bills which in line with the above-mentioned decrees would create a mortgage system based on private land-ownership as well as a title registry for real property following the example of the German/Austrian "Grundbuch".

8. Financial Sector

Ukraine's banking system and its capital market are both still in an embryonic stage; nevertheless reforms towards a viable banking system and capital market are proceeding, some with noticeable success.

8.1. Banking

In accordance with established international practice, Ukraine has a two-tier banking system distinguishing between central bank activity and commercial banking operations.

8.1.1. *National Bank of Ukraine* (NBU)

Central bank functions are vested in the National Bank of Ukraine (NBU) which was created in 1992 and has since enjoyed relative independence. As usual in transition economies, the NBU carries out both Ukraine's monetary policy and the supervision of Ukraine's banking system.

As regards its monetary policy, the NBU has achieved remarkable success. Inflation has been brought down to some 10 per cent in 1998 from over 10 000 per cent in mid-1993. The hryvnya has proven remarkably stable since its introduction in 1996, with an initial equivalent of some 1.7 hryvnya to $1 and a ratio of some 5.40 hryvnya to $1 in May 2000. Given the chronic liquidity squeeze of both the public and the private sectors in Ukraine and, especially the high arrears on wages and pensions, this record demonstrates that the NBU has succeeded in withstanding political pressures for soft money.

Banking supervision is carried out through a graduated system of licenses, requiring licenses for both the establishment of a commercial bank and for particular banking activities. Licenses are granted only if specified conditions are met and can be revoked in case of subsequent violations. Requirements for banks and banking operations in 1998 and 1999 have been tightened in line with international standards. Thus, since January 1998, the minimum capital requirement for banks was increased to 1 million Euro.

In December 1997, capital and risk regulations were introduced in accordance with BIS norms (*e.g.*, maximum exposure to a single borrower and to the aggregate large credit exposure; maximum loans per single insider and to all insiders; maximum outstanding interbank loans; refunding ratio limited to 300 per cent of bank capital; and equity investment and non-state debt limited to 50 per cent of capital). Since February 1998, commercial banks are furthermore required to maintain accounts and be audited in accordance with International Accountancy Standards (IAS). Under the 1997 Corporate Tax Law, provisioning of non-performing loans is encouraged.[36]

In May 1999, the Law on the National Bank of Ukraine was adopted, which sets out the organisational structure of the National Bank, defines the powers of the NBU and provides specific standards for banking supervision, money transfers and other matters. According to the new law, the NBU is politically independent, economically autonomous and committed to transparency of the banking system. It may neither cover the budget deficit through direct lending nor issue treasury bills.

The reference to independence of the NBU notwithstanding, the new law creates a "Council of the NBU" whose members represent political constituencies of Ukraine.[37] The Council is authorised to develop major principles of monetary policy, make recommendations to the NBU Board on regulatory and monetary measures as well as exchange rate and currency regulation policies, and to approve or veto decisions of the Board. While the Council thus enjoys considerable powers, its accountability is not defined.

8.1.2. *Commercial Banks*

In early 2000, the NBU had licensed 163 commercial banks. They include five big state-owned and 180 privately owned banks. While accounting for some 50 per cent of the entire turnover in this sector, the state banks report only some 28 per cent of overall profits, indicating that they are operating less efficiently than privately owned banks. The overall volume of banking capital in Ukraine amounted in early 2000 to some UAH5.9 billion, *i.e.* less than the assets of a small bank in Western Europe.

While marginally effective in facilitating payments (even though settlements are frequently subject to cumbersome and lengthy procedures), banks still play only a limited role as intermediaries of savings (collecting deposits from the public and using them to finance business operations). In terms of Ukraine's GDP, commercial bank lending was 8.6 and 9.3 per cent of GDP in 1998 and 1999 respectively. About one third of loans, equal to 2 per cent of GDP, are considered to be non-performing.

To build confidence in the banking sector and promote its financial intermediary role, a draft bill on "Banks and Banking" is pending in the Parliament and had its first reading in June 2000. The bill defines the types of banks to be admitted in Ukraine and sets out requirements and standards concerning their management structure as well as their operational and financial policies. While liberalising banking operations in some respects, the bill retains limitations for activities of foreign banks in Ukraine, notably the prohibition of carrying out banking operations in Ukraine through branch offices.

As of early 2000, eight foreign banks were operating in Ukraine and many others maintained representative offices. Previous discriminations against foreign banks have been eliminated. Since July 1997, foreign banks, through affiliates incorporated in Ukraine, are allowed to carry out banking operations in hryvnya; and since January 1998 they are subject to the same minimum capital requirements as Ukrainian-owned banks. The application of international accounting standards to the banking sector has furthermore paved the way to foreign bank involvement.

8.2. Capital Market

The Ukrainian securities market has failed to develop into the source of financing for companies that need capital. Instead, it serves as a means to consolidate control over strategic enterprises. Most of the trading is done offshore (up to 90 per cent).[38] The laws governing the securities market are both outdated and numerous, and need to be streamlined. With the recent economic growth and the accelerated privatisation of lucrative enterprises the time has come to restructure the securities market in order to repatriate the trading and to create a securities market capable of providing the badly needed capital investment for Ukraine's companies.

As of early 2000, the capital market in Ukraine remained even less developed than the banking sector. Nonetheless, considerable efforts are under way on developing capital markets and some remarkable successes should be noted.

8.2.1. Structure

A concept adopted by Parliament in September 1995 envisaged capital markets based on decentralisation and Government control. In June 1995 the State Commission for Securities and Stock Markets (SSMSC) was created as an independent agency under the President and accountable to the Parliament; in 1996, the SSMSC was given primary responsibility for developing the Ukrainian capital markets and exercise state control over them. Since then, a two-level regulatory system has emerged, combining state control and self-regulation of market organisations and professional associations.

Until mid-1995, stockholdings had been registered by the issuers themselves maintaining registry books for that purpose. This practice offered a potential for abuse; and it was in 1996 replaced by a system of independent registrars licensed by the SSMSC.

In 1999, the SSMSC established the "National Depository of Ukraine" as the focal point of the national securities depository system. Organised as a joint stock company with the State and leading market participants as its shareholders, the National Depository has developed a depository system, introduced a unified accounting of deposits, and facilitates the co-ordination of the Ukrainian with the international depository systems. The present system comprises the National

Depository, local depositories, custodians (banks and securities traders) and registrars of securities holders.[39]

8.2.2. Markets

There exist two market systems in Ukraine – traditional stock exchanges and alternative over-the-counter trading systems.

The initial concept envisaged markets based on traditional stock exchanges. As of September 2000, there exist seven stock exchanges – three in Kiev and four in different regions of Ukraine. With the exception the Kiev based Ukrainian Stock Exchange (the largest and oldest stock exchange in Ukraine), trading focuses mainly on the initial placing of shares of privatised companies; the secondary market is still underdeveloped. In 1999 all seven stock exchanges together accounted for only some ten per cent of total turnover on both the primary and secondary markets.

The bulk of transactions is carried out in an alternative trading system, namely the "Ukrainian First Trading System" (FSTS), which is a non-governmental member-governed association of licensed Ukrainian securities traders. The FSTS has set up an electronic trading information network similar to the NASDAQ system in the United States. Established in July 1996 with the assistance of USAID, it dominates the Ukrainian securities market, accounting for almost 90 per cent of total trade. The FSTS publishes its information daily; it has developed a rating system of securities listed in this market; and in 1997 it has created the "FSTS Technical Centre", the primary securities trading and information centre in Ukraine.

The two oldest associations of securities traders are: the "Ukrainian Association of Investment Business" (UAIB), including investment funds, investment companies and securities traders; and the "Professional Association of Registrars and Depositories" (PARD), comprising independent registrars, depositories and commercial banks that provide depository services.

8.3. Accounting and Auditing

The old Ukrainian accounting system was established by Cabinet regulations of April 1993. It focused on reporting for tax purposes and did not provide relevant information to capital markets, management and creditors. In July 1999 the Rada passed and in August 1999 President Kuchma signed a new law "On Accounting and Financial Reporting in Ukraine". The law states that the financial accounting system is to be based on Ukrainian Accounting Standards (UAS), which are not to contradict international standards.

The new UAS are an improvement over the old Soviet-style accounting system. However, it remains unclear how the first 17 UAS, and future UAS planned for 2000 and 2001, will be applied in practice by both the accounting firms and companies. Under the partially developed UAS, potential investors and creditors will find it difficult to fully understand financial statements prepared by Ukrainian enterprises. Both investors and creditors will have to translate UAS into national and international reference points. Companies are still required to produce two separate sets of accounts, one for tax purposes, the other for financial reporting. Many enterprises continue to focus on accounting for tax purposes.

Since 1998, banks are required to produce financial reports in accordance with NBU regulations, which are based on IAS. Enterprises with foreign investments usually operate with two accounting systems, one in accordance with Ukrainian requirements and the other one in accordance with the reporting obligations of their parent companies. This leads to considerable administrative expenses and creates complexity in the application of double taxation agreements and tax credit systems under parent companies' tax laws.

Ukrainian audited financial statements have limited international credibility. Compulsory audits can only be performed by Ukrainian auditors. International auditing firms are not allowed to sign statutory audit reports. Since 1 January 1999, the Audit Chamber of Ukraine has approved 32 auditing standards and the Code of Professional Ethics for Ukrainian Auditors, which must be followed by all certified auditors. International Standards on Auditing, as developed by the International Federation of Accountants (IFAC), are not applied by certified auditors in Ukraine.

The accounting and auditing professions have been developing rapidly in Ukraine since 1998. With the involvement of large western accounting firms and foreign assistance programmes, knowledge of international accounting methods is becoming widespread. However, a number of practical problems exist. Most tax and financial accountants have little training in the use of the new systems. In addition, public and private sector structures needed to regulate the accounting and auditing profession are still emerging.

9. Trade and Currency Regimes

9.1. Trade Regime

The ground rules of foreign trade activities are laid down in the Law "On Foreign Economic Activities" of July 1991. While addressing a myriad of trans-border business activities, such as international financial operations and securities trading, foreign investment relations and currency trading, this law mainly serves as the legal basis of export-import operations. In early 2001, a new comprehensive customs code is pending in the Rada.

Together with a set of supporting Government and NBU resolutions, the Foreign Economic Activities Law in principle establishes a liberal trade regime under which every Ukrainian resident may sell any products/services abroad or purchase them from abroad. Import/export contracts, as any other contracts under the Foreign Economic Activities Law, may provide for international arbitration.

However, registration requirements apply to numerous types of arrangements with foreign parties, notably barter and counter-trade contracts, contracts of state enterprises, and joint investment agreements. For a few commodities, a system of "indicative prices" is imposed; Ukrainian customs decline clearance of such goods if those price levels are not observed.[40] This system is, for instance, applied where Ukraine faces antidumping measures or investigations.

9.1.1. Exports

In the Soviet Union and the first years of post independent Ukraine, exports were subject to stringent quota and licensing systems. Since 1994 most of these restrictions have been abolished. As of spring 2000, quotas and licensing requirements remain only for few products, chiefly military commodities and "dual-use" goods. Previously widespread export duties were also limited to few product lines; and no value added tax is levied on exports (except on exports to Russia where pursuant to the Free Trade Agreement between Russia and Ukraine, VAT is charged on exports but not on imports in the destination country).

9.1.2. Imports

Import restrictions apply to specified products, namely weapons, narcotics, chemical and hazardous substances, certain pharmaceutical and communications related products, sunflower and soy oil. As a rule imports are subject to:

- an import VAT of 20 per cent.
- excise taxes for the importation of certain luxury products such as tobacco products, alcoholic beverages, motor vehicles (up to 300 per cent); and
- customs fees.

Some imports are exempted from import VAT, especially imports from the Russian Federation (under the Free Trade Agreement), imports contributed to enterprises as foreign investments, and imports into some free economic zones.

As Ukraine is not (yet) a member of the World Trade Organisation (WTO), its import tariffs are not bound under the WTO system. No import duties are levied on imports from countries with which Ukraine has concluded free trade agreements, mainly CIS countries (see Annex I), and reduced rates apply to a large number of countries with which Ukraine has concluded most favoured nation treatment agreements.

Non-tariff trade barriers still impede imports into Ukraine. Most notable used to be restrictions on the import of agricultural products and used cars; the latter were relaxed in March 2000.

Considerable non-tariff barriers still result from the imposition of technical standards and certification requirements on many imports by the "State Committee for Standardisation of Ukraine" (Derzhstandart). Even though Ukraine is a member of various international standardisation bodies, such as the International Standards Organisation (ISO), it usually fails to recognise foreign product certificates even if issued in line with international standards (unless recognition is provided in an international treaty of Ukraine). Draft legislation with the aim of improving the situation is presently pending in the Rada. Certification procedures of Derzhstandart are reported to be non-transparent, lengthy and unusually expensive; for many products, pre-market certification procedures have been established requiring mandatory visits of Derzhstandart officials to exporting factories at exporters' expense.[41]

9.1.3. International Arrangements

- WTO Accession

Since December 1993 negotiations are under way on Ukraine's accession to the WTO). Ukraine intends to join WTO in 2001 or 2002. In order to qualify for WTO membership, however, considerable work still lies ahead. In particular Ukraine will have to:

- negotiate market access agreements, including tariff reductions with WTO members;
- develop an institutional and administrative system to ensure proper implementation of staged reductions of tariffs in line with Ukraine's commitments (bindings) in conformity with the obligations of national treatment;
- eliminate any discriminatory excise taxes on imported goods;
- bring its non-tariff trade regulations into compliance with WTO requirements, especially its certification and standardisation system and its sanitary and phytosanitary norms;
- eliminate any remaining quantitative import restrictions;
- revise its system of state subsidies in the agricultural sector;

- proceed with liberalising services in accordance with the commitments undertaken by Ukraine pursuant to the General Agreement in Trade and Services (GATTS);

- reform its customs regulations system (*e.g.*, customs regulation practices and other aspects of customs legislation);

- improve the protection of intellectual property in accordance with the Agreement on Trade Related Aspects of Intellectual Property Rights (TRIPS);

- review the role of state trading enterprises and other entities with exclusive or special privileges; and

- bring its regional agreements in line with relevant WTO disciplines, in particular GATT Article XXIV.

- *Partnership and Co-operation Agreement with the European Union* (PCA)

Even though Ukraine has not yet acceded to the WTO, many WTO disciplines are already binding on Ukraine in relation to the European Union and its Member States due to the PCA. These disciplines include the principles of most favoured nation treatment (Article 10 of the PCA), national treatment of exports with respect to internal taxes and other charges (Article 15), adequacy of testing, registration and certification charges of imports (Article 16 of the PCA), freedom of transit of goods (Article 11) and prohibition of quantitative import restrictions (Article 14).

The PCA is asymmetric in favour of Ukraine in one important point. By virtue of the most favoured nation principle, Ukrainian exports to the European Union benefit from all tariff concessions that the European Union has made under the WTO/GATT system, while its tariffs on imports from the European Union are not yet bound. This means that Ukraine is still free to raise its tariffs in order to protect domestic industries.

This privilege would be forgone if Ukraine entered into a free trade area with the European Union, as envisaged by the PCA (Article 4). A first feasibility study on such a free trade area has been undertaken and negotiations are presently under way. Ukraine is furthermore seeking association status with the European Union, which would require a gradual reduction of its tariffs on European Union imports.[42]

- *Free Trade Agreements*

Ukraine has concluded bilateral free trade agreements with all CIS and Baltic countries except Kyrgyzstan and Tajikistan. Ukraine is also a party to the Free Trade Zone Agreement signed by CIS members in April 1995. Although ambitious in principle, this agreement continues to be poorly implemented. Negotiations towards a regional free trade agreement are under way in the framework of the Black See Economic Co-operation (BSEC) to which Ukraine is a party along with Albania, Armenia, Azerbaijan, Bulgaria, Georgia, Greece, Moldova, Romania, Russia and Turkey.[43] Ukraine also intends to accede to the Central European Free Trade Agreement (CEFTA) after joining the WTO.

Ukraine has furthermore concluded trade agreements with some 12 countries, including some industrial countries.[44] These agreements grant on a reciprocal basis most favoured nation status to export-import operations with the countries concerned. As in the case of the PCA, Ukraine benefits via these agreements from the tariff concessions made by its partner countries in the WTO/GATT framework without having bound its own tariffs.

9.2. Currency Regulations

Through Presidential Decree of August 1996 the hryvnya (UAH) was introduced as Ukraine's national currency, replacing the previous karbovantsi at a rate of 100 000:1. All settlement of accounts and payments in Ukraine must be carried out in hryvnya only; in practice, however, prices are frequently quoted in dollars and then converted into hryvnya for payment purposes at the prevailing exchange rate.

Until the end of 1996 the hryvnya was set to fluctuate against the $ within a corridor of 1.7 to 1.9. Subsequently, the corridor was expanded several times up to 3.4 to 4.6 in 1999. In February 2000, it was abandoned altogether, and, the UAH in theory is now floating freely at around 5.4 in March 2001 (even though still managed by the NBU).

Until March 1999, the official rate of the hryvnya was set by the NBU on the basis of auctions at the Ukrainian Interbank Currency Exchange. Since then, the official rate is determined at the Interbank Currency Market of Ukraine. The NBU no longer fixes a rate, but continues to exercise some influence by intervening in market operations.

In May 1997, Ukraine introduced the convertibility of the UAH for current operations in accordance with Article VIII of the IMF Articles of Agreement. As a consequence, non-residents are now allowed to open bank accounts in Ukraine in local and foreign currency on the same conditions as Ukrainian residents; and they may purchase foreign currency in Ukraine's currency market through authorised banks. Authorised banks may buy and sell foreign currency freely at the Ukrainian Interbank Currency Market.

Under the 1996 Foreign Investment Law, foreign investors are guaranteed the free transfer of dividends and other investment proceeds, upon payment of taxes and other fiscal charges. There are at present no restrictions on the repatriation of investment proceeds; and foreign currency can be freely bought from authorised commercial banks at the prevailing market rate.

In response to the Russian financial crisis several currency regulations were introduced in 1998, notably the following:

- Ukrainian exporters must sell 50 per cent of their export proceeds in hard currency to the NBU;

- Ukrainian residents may not maintain bank accounts outside Ukraine without NBU license;

- all residents must declare their currency holdings abroad and file monthly reports on their foreign currency operations;

- all currency operations within Ukraine must be carried out through a Ukrainian bank licensed to perform currency operations;

- Ukrainian resident employees may be paid in Ukrainian currency only.[45]

In January 2000, access to foreign currency was liberalised – banks were permitted to make foreign currency loans, and earlier restrictions on purchasing currency in Ukraine to service currency loans were repealed. Enterprises with foreign investments established between March 1992 and March 1996 were furthermore exempted from the above-mentioned mandatory sale of export proceeds, and other enterprises were permitted to apply for the same exemption.

10. Privatisation and Enterprise Re-organisation (Bankruptcy)

10.1. Privatisation

10.1.1. 1992-99 Programmes

The first privatisation program was launched in March 1992 with three laws, a law on the so-called large-scale privatisation (the "Privatisation Law"), a law on the privatisation of small enterprises (the "Law on Small Privatisation") and a law on the privatisation through privatisation certificates (the "Privatisation Certificate Law"). To implement these laws, annual privatisation programmes were adopted by Parliament in 1992, 1994, 1997, 1998 and 1999. These programmes were administered by the "State Property Fund" (the SPF), created for this purpose in 1992 under the joint control of President and Parliament.

79

Privatisation has proceeded on the basis of the four main methods outlined below:

i) the transfer of enterprises to their previous managements and/or employee collectives under buy-out plans; this method was mainly used for small enterprises;

ii) the conversion of privatisation and compensation certificates in shares in state enterprises after the latter had been reorganised as joint stock companies (corporatisation);[46]

iii) the sale of state enterprises at auctions or through tender proceedings to the highest bidders (so-called "commercial tenders"); and

iv) the sale of state enterprises to strategic investors which offered the best business plan and most investments to rehabilitate the enterprise (so-called "non-commercial" tenders).

Over the years, the focus shifted from voucher to cash privatisation and from commercial to non-commercial tenders.

By the end of 1998, certificate privatisation as well as privatisation of small enterprises had been largely completed, with some 80 to 90 per cent of such enterprises being privatised. Nonetheless, over 80 per cent of the value of assets in the industrial and utilities sectors still remained in the public sector. These assets are mainly held by some 200 largest state enterprises, which are not yet privatised.

The involvement of foreign investors in the first rounds of privatisation was minimal. Until 1997 they were deterred by a requirement to pay the purchase price in hard currency calculated on the basis of a fictitious and highly discriminatory conversion rate. While this requirement was eliminated in 1998, administrative obstacles and non-transparent procedures have continued to discourage foreign investors from participating in the privatisation process.

10.1.2. 2000-2002 Programmes

In December 1999, the President issued a Decree "On Urgent Measures for Acceleration of Privatisation of Property in Ukraine" (the "Acceleration Decree") setting out the privatisation targets for 2000-2002. With a focus on the privatisation of large and medium size enterprises, the Decree envisages reaping some $3 billion from privatisation during this period (for comparison: in 1999, some $150 million were generated).

Under the Decree, privatisation efforts will primarily target long-term strategic investors, and foreign investors in particular. Towards this end:

- shares will be sold in the largest blocks possible;

- enterprises will be reorganised and debt restructured (*i.e.*, investors will no longer be required to assume all pre-existing debt and maintain all "social" facilities of the enterprises);

- favourable conditions will be offered to strategic investors;

- investment obligations will in certain cases be waived for strategic foreign investors; and

- the protection of minority shareholders is supposed to improved.

Special privatisation programmes will be launched for the energy sector (sale of 11 companies to strategic investors) and the telecommunications sector (privatisation of some 50 per cent of UkrTeleCom while 50 per cent plus 1 share will be retained by the State). A significant number of enterprises is still considered to be of strategic importance for Ukraine and therefore reserved for continued state ownership. The list of reserved enterprises is a subject of heated political debate.

10.1.3. *Land Privatisation*

Stalled land privatisation is frequently cited among the impediments to FDI in Ukraine. Privatisation of land only started in December 1999. Previously it was blocked by the restrictive regulations of the still existing Land Code; and earlier Presidential decrees attempting land privatisation in specific problem areas (such as a Decree of January 1999 allowing the sale of land under uncompleted constructions sites) had remained without significant effect.

In late 1999 and early 2000, the President issued two land privatisation decrees, one for agricultural and the other for industrial land. The Decree "On Urgent Measures for the Acceleration of Reforms in the Agricultural Sector of the Economy" of December 1999 aims at developing the agricultural sector on the principles of private ownership. It entitles members of agricultural collectives to obtain a portion of the land and share of the other property of the collective as private property.

In February 2000, a Presidential Decree followed permitting the transfer of non-agricultural land to Ukrainian citizens and companies. However, this decree – like the 1992 Land Code – explicitly excludes foreigners from owning Ukrainian land, limiting them to the lease of industrial land. It remains unclear whether enterprises with foreign investments incorporated under Ukrainian law are considered as Ukrainian corporate citizens and as such may acquire land-ownership under the Decree.

81

10.2. Bankruptcy Legislation

Privatisation of large state enterprises depends on effective bankruptcy/reorganisation mechanisms. Such enterprises are typically burdened with huge debt, notably tax arrears accumulated under prior confiscatory rates. Moreover, hardly any of these enterprises as a whole operates at the profit. Privatisation therefore appears to be possible in practice only if *i*) such enterprises are reorganised in a way that non-viable operations are closed down and viable ones are offered for sale and *ii*) buyers are not required to assume the entire debt burden of the privatised state enterprise.

10.2.1. *Previous Bankruptcy Regime*

Until the end of 1999, bankruptcy proceedings were governed by the Law "On Bankruptcy" of May 1992 as amended in 1993, 1994 and 1995. Deficiencies of this law virtually ensured its ineffectiveness, including the following:

- enterprise reorganisations initiated by the debtor were not envisaged at all;
- creditors could file for bankruptcy proceedings only after lengthy and costly procedures;
- no mechanisms were provided for enterprise restructuring;
- the law left only a choice between liquidation and so-called "sanitation" of the enterprise, with sanitation requiring an outside "sanitor" (investor) to agree to assume all debts of the enterprise in exchange for ownership.

Despite these and other deficiencies of bankruptcy legislation, bankruptcy cases increased rapidly from 6 562 in 1996 to 12 281 in 1998. However, most of these proceedings were initiated by tax authorities; many of them were also a result of Ukrainian tax legislation allowing writing off bad debts only upon a court decision that a debtor is bankrupt. Hardly any bankruptcy proceedings were carried out in the context of privatisation.[47]

10.2.2. *New Bankruptcy Law*

In June 1999, a new Bankruptcy Law was adopted and entered into force on 1 January 2000.

The new law provides a more sophisticated framework for bankruptcy reorganisation proceedings than previous legislation, responding to some, albeit not all reform proposals. It in particular:

- allows debtors to initiate bankruptcy reorganisation procedures, thus enabling the reorganisation of state enterprises for privatisation purposes;
- makes reorganisation the first choice, with liquidation the last resort;
- offers rather flexible reorganisation procedures;

- permits amicable settlements between the debtor-in-bankruptcy and its creditors;

- provides for a moratorium on debt payments by the debtor upon opening of bankruptcy proceedings with a view to facilitating reorganisations and ensuring proportional satisfaction of all creditors; and

- introduces simplified procedures for the recognition of undisputed claims.

However, as with the previous bankruptcy legislation, creditors can only file bankruptcy proceedings if they have "indisputable claims", *i.e.* claims confirmed by a court decision. This requires creditors to go through lengthy and expensive proceedings even where their claims are undisputed and the debtor's insolvency is obvious. The new law reportedly includes some inconsistencies with the draft Civil Code; upon adoption of the latter these would have to be eliminated.

Bankruptcy proceedings are carried out by the *arbitrazh* courts, thus suffering from both the lack of expertise on the part of *arbitrazh* court judges and the insecurity about the future of *arbitrazh* courts pending the reorganisation of the court system.

11. Public Governance and Competition

11.1. Public Governance

Complaints of investors in Ukraine abound about lengthy, cumbersome and non-transparent administrative procedures with unpredictable results, a high level of corruption, and a distortion of competition through state intervention, direct and indirect, in business operations.

On the basis of its "Business Environment and Enterprise Performance Survey", the EBRD compares investors' perception of Ukraine's public governance with that of 19 other CIS and CEE countries.[48] According to the EBRD, "state capture", *i.e.*, the undue influence of powerful vested interests in the economy, in Ukraine is the second highest of all the countries surveyed;[49] and the influence of privileged firms on the state is in Ukraine even the highest of all the 20 states compared.[50] State intervention in enterprise decisions is also considered to be exceptionally high in Ukraine, with Ukraine being rated as the second most interventionist state of the 20.[51] Along with the high degree of state intervention in the economy comes the highest "time tax" in the 20 countries, *i.e.*, the time which enterprise managements spend on interacting with Government bureaucracies (in Ukraine more than 17 per cent of overall management time).[52] Bribes paid to officials in Ukraine finally are reported to average to about 6.5 per cent of enterprises' annual revenues, the fourth highest percentage of the 20 states after the three Trans-Caucasian countries.[53]

The perceived flaws of public governance in Ukraine reflect systemic weaknesses of existing administrative structures. To begin with, the public sector in Ukraine is bloated at all levels of the state – central government, *oblast* administrations and municipal administrations. Until the end 1999, there existed more than 90 ministries and state agencies and committees with the rank of a ministry. Many line ministries, committees and agencies still pursued functions of economic planning and purposefully interfered in economic activities, often representing vested interests (like, for example, the Ministry for Industrial Policies, Committee on Material Reserves, Leasing Fund, State Clearing Committee).

Government officials are grossly underpaid by international standards, with a medium monthly salary clustering between $100 and 200 at the end of 1999. The combination of interventionist authority, wide and often unclear discretionary powers and low pay explains the lamented deficiencies in the integrity and competence of the Ukrainian public service.

While the picture might still look bleak in spring 2000, institutional reforms are under way to remedy these problems. In December 1999, the Cabinet reduced its staff by 25 per cent, signalling the start of decisive reform; and in early 2000 the total number of ministries, committees and agencies was reduced to 46, *i.e.* by some 50 per cent. According to a Cabinet resolution of April 2000, some 20 000 employees of the remaining 46 ministries, etc., were terminated; and by the end of 2000 some 300 000 government workers were intended to be laid off.

Probably more important than downsizing Government bureaucracy is refocusing its functions from economic planning towards creating and ensuring framework conditions for market operations. Again, first steps in this direction have already been made. The above-mentioned closures affected mainly interventionist line ministries, committees and agencies (such as the Ministries of Industrial Policies, Coal and Mining, Foreign Economic Relations and Trade, the State Investment Clearing Committee) while the role of market institutions (Antimonopoly Committee, SSMSC, State Property Fund, Bankruptcy Agency and State Accounting Chamber) remained unaffected.[54]

While important, institutional reforms alone are not sufficient to make Ukrainian bureaucracy business friendly. They must be supplemented by new administrative procedures that introduce simplicity and transparency, reduce officials' discretionary powers, enhance officials' accountability and strengthen judicial protection against misuse of powers. As barter trade facilitates both corruption and tax evasion, reforms must also be designed with a view to encouraging cash transactions instead of barter trade.

11.1.1. Business Registration Procedures

To set up an enterprise in Ukraine and undertake business operations requires a host of different registrations and permits. Any new enterprise must be registered with the local state administration under the 1991 law "On Entrepreneurship" and implementing Government regulations; foreign investments must additionally be registered as such with local authorities under the 1996 Foreign Investment Law. Moreover, all investments in excess of $100 000 and representing more than 25 per cent of the equity in an enterprise require moreover approval of the Antimonopoly Committee. Further licenses and permits are required for special sectors (banking, insurance, broadcasting, publishing houses, etc.) and special types of operations (export/import licenses for certain product lines, currency transactions, etc.).

Such registrations, licenses and permits are issued by officials who with preference follow internal and publicly unavailable instructions rather than provisions of relevant legislation. Incidents were reported where officials created requirements in addition to those established in the law, such as a mandatory contribution to the social fund of the registration body. Time limits established in the relevant legislation (such as a five working day limit for registering an enterprise under Article 8 of the Law on Entrepreneurship) are regularly exceeded.[55]

Registration practices vary remarkably among Ukrainian cities and even the districts of one city. In Kiev, for instance, some companies are reported to avoid certain districts only because of cumbersome registration practices.

Amendments to the Law on Entrepreneurship of December 1997 and a Cabinet Resolution of July 1998 limited the number of business activities subject to licenses (51 as of April 1999) and simplified registration procedures. While previously entrepreneurs had to register individually with the State Statistics Committee, the State Tax Administration, the Pension fund and the social security fund, they now register only once with the local administration which in turn transmits this information to the other bodies. As a result of these simplifications, the average time to receive a license decreased from 35 days in 1997 to 14 days in 1998/1999.[56]

11.1.2. Business Inspections

In addition to regulatory restrictions on entry and other factors that deter business, inspections of enterprises by state agencies (i.e. tax administration, fire department and police) still considerably interrupt business operations and absorb substantial management time. Both the number and the length of inspections vary noticeably among regions, reflecting the wide discretion of administrative authorities.

85

Until 1997 any monitoring body had the power to inspect any enterprise, at any time, for almost any reason and without warning. This power was restricted by the 1999 Presidential Decree on Deregulation limiting financial inspections to one planned inspection per year, requiring all planned financial inspections to take place at the same time and specifying the conditions for unplanned inspections. As a result, inspections of small enterprises declined sharply from an average of 78 in 1997 to 3 in the last quarter of 1998.[57]

11.2. Competition

11.2.1. Legislative Framework

A package of three laws (Antimonopoly Law, Unfair Competition Law and Law on the Antimonopoly Committee), Cabinet decrees and Antimonopoly Committee regulations adopted between 1992 and 1997 establishes a relatively advanced framework for developing a competitive market in Ukraine. The system is administered by the Antimonopoly Commission (the "AMC") created for that purpose in 1993 under the joint control of Parliament and President.

The AMC enjoys rather broad enforcement powers combining comprehensive pre-establishment and pre-merger approval requirements, sanctions for violations of the antimonopoly/unfair competition laws and the power to break up existing monopolies. Its powers include the authority to bring actions against state authorities discriminating against particular market participants in favour of others. Of special importance is the role of the AMC in the privatisation process where it is charged with preventing state monopolies from becoming private ones.

The caseload prosecuted by the AMC has increased steadily since the Commission's creation. In 1998, it prosecuted some 1 700 violations mainly related to restrictions on the purchase of particular commodities, the imposition of illegal taxes and so-called forced contracts. In the latter cases, state authorities had pressed private businesses to enter into contracts with unnecessary intermediaries between the state administration and users of government services or to obtain mandatory insurance from a specific company.

In general, the AMC appears to be playing a beneficial role in challenging anti-competitive private and public conduct that discourages investment and undermines the efficiency of a market-economy. The low thresholds for pre-establishment and pre-merger reviews as well as ambiguities relating to the procedure for appeals against AMC decisions to the courts are subjects of continued criticism.[58]

11.2.2. Major Distortions of Competition

Despite the relatively advanced stage of competition/antimonopoly legislation and its enforcement, the Ukrainian market is still far away from a level playing field with undistorted competition. Major distortions result from direct and indirect subsidisation of preferred enterprises, especially remaining state enterprises, as well as the huge shadow economy.

• *State Subsidies*

State subsidies to enterprises are estimated to amount to some 20 per cent of Ukrainian gross domestic product, surpassing by far relevant levels of magnitude in mature market economies and Central European transition economies. While direct subsidies have decreased in recent years, indirect or implicit subsidies have considerably increased.

Direct subsidies, defined as capital transfers from the budget to enterprises for the financing as current expenditures, played a key role in the central economic planning of the FSU and the first year of Ukrainian independence (1991) when they amounted to some 46 per cent of the budget or 15 per cent of GDP. Thereafter they were gradually scaled back – from 14.5 per cent of GDP in 1994 to 4.7 per cent in 1995 and 2.2 per cent in 1998. By comparison, corresponding figures in Central and Eastern Europe cluster between 1.7 and 4.4 per cent of GDP. Subsidisation was largely achieved through special funds, such as the State Material Reserve Fund under the Cabinet of Ministers, the Innovation Fund and the Chernobyl Fund.

While direct subsidies thus have come down to "normal" levels, indirect or implicit subsidies are on the rise notably:

– tax preferences granted to preferred enterprises such as shipbuilding and locally produced automobiles (in 1997 estimated at 2.2 per cent of GDP);

– non-payment of taxes, social security and other fiscal charges with arrears of enterprises estimated at some 12,7 per cent of GDP in January 1998, roughly three times those in Poland;

– tax write-offs and tax restructuring for certain enterprises and sectors, estimated to cluster around US$5.4 billion in 1997;

– other indirect subsidies, such as targeted credits authorised by the Government or Government guarantees (*e.g.* for sugar and ship-building industries);

– granting of monopoly rights for production and services (*e.g.* access to foreign data transmission networks exclusively through the network of UkrTeleCom, Ukrkosmos, Inforcom, premises leased free of charge by local authorities to preferred enterprises).

To an increasing extent, competition is also distorted by tax and customs privileges granted to enterprises in free economic zones, which sell their production in Ukrainian markets. The subsidisation practices are non-transparent, thus nurturing bureaucracy, corruption and distortions of competition.[59]

The dismal picture notwithstanding, major recent reforms to downsize subsidies and curb resulting distortions must be recognised. The budget for 2000 for the first time provides for no deficit, achieved mainly though a drastic reduction of subsidies. In May 2000, tax privileges of some 150 state enterprises were annulled.

It should also be noted that most of the enterprises and agencies closed down in early 2000 were just the ones mainly engaged in the distribution of subsidies.

- *Shadow Economy*

As noted before, the shadow economy in Ukraine is estimated to cluster somewhere between 50 and 70 per cent of official GDP. Enterprises operating in the shadow economy enjoy *de facto* exemption from taxation, social contributions and Government regulations (*e.g.*, environmental protection, and worker safety standards). Effective taxation as well as the cost of compliance with Government regulations is exceptionally high in Ukraine, explaining both incentives for enterprises to go underground and the magnitude of competitive advantages of enterprises in the shadow economy over their competitors in the formal economy.[60]

The costs and risks associated with going into the shadow economy are as a rule much higher for foreign investors than for domestic ones. Exposure to competition from a large and increasing shadow economy therefore strongly discourages foreign investment.

Abbreviations

AMC	Antimonopoly Committee of Ukraine
BIS	Bank for International Settlements
BIT	Bilateral Investment Protection Treaty
BSEC	Black Sea Economic Co-operation
CEE countries	Central and Eastern European countries
CEFTA	Central European Free Trade Agreement
CIS	Commonwealth of Independent States (which includes as full or associate members all countries of the former Soviet Union, except the Baltic States)
ECT	Energy Charter Treaty of 1994
EU	European Union
FDI	Foreign Direct Investment
FIAC	Foreign Investment Advisory Council
FSTS	Ukrainian First Trading System
GATT	General Agreement on Tariffs and Trade
GATS	General Agreement on Trade in Services
GDP	Gross Domestic Product
IAS	International Accounting Standards
ICSID	International Centre for Settlement of Investment Disputes
ICSID Convention	Convention on the Settlement of Investment Disputes between States and Nationals of other States
IMF	International Monetary Fund
ISO	International Standardization Organization
NADEI	National Agency for Development and European Integration of Ukraine
NBU	National Bank of Ukraine
PCA	Partnership and Co-operation Agreement between Ukraine and the European Union
PDA	Priority Development Area
Review	The Investment Policy Review for Ukraine, OECD December 2000
SEZ	Special Economic Zone
SMEs	Small and Medium-Sized Enterprises

SPF	State Property Fund
SSMSC	State Commission for Securities and Stock Market of Ukraine
TRIPS	Agreement on Trade Related Aspects of Intellectual Property Rights
UAH	Hryvnya (national currency of Ukraine since 1996)
UAS	Ukrainian Accounting Standards
USAID	United States Agency for International Development
WTO	World Trade Organisation

Law of Ukraine "On the Regime of Foreign Investment"

With changes and additions per the Law of Ukraine of July 16, 1999 No. 997-XIV and June 08, 2000 No.1807-III. Proceeding from the goals, principles and provisions of the legislation of Ukraine, this Law determines specific features of regime of foreign investments on the territory of Ukraine.

Section I. General Provisions

Article 1. Definition of Terms Used in the Law

The terms used in this Law have the following meanings:

1) foreign investors – entities that carry out investment activity on the territory of Ukraine, namely: legal entities, established under legislation other than the legislation of Ukraine; foreign natural persons who have no permanent residence on the territory of Ukraine and are not limited in their legal capacity; foreign states, international governmental and non-governmental organisations; other foreign subjects of investment activity recognised as such by effective legislation of Ukraine.

2) Foreign investments – valuables invested by foreign investors in objects of investment activity pursuant to effective legislation of Ukraine for the purpose of gaining profit or achieving social effect;

3) Enterprise with foreign investments – an enterprise (organisation) of any legal organisational form, established in compliance with Ukrainian legislation, where foreign investments in its charter fund, if available, constitute no less than 10 per cent.

Enterprise acquires the status of an enterprise with foreign investments from the date of entering foreign investment into accounting records;

Article 2. Types of Foreign Investments

Foreign investments can be contributed in the form of:

- foreign currency recognised as convertible by the National Bank of Ukraine;
- the currency of Ukraine if reinvesting in the object of initial investment or in any other objects of investment in accordance with Ukrainian legislation on the condition of payment of tax on profit (incomes);
- any personal and real property and property rights related thereto;

- stocks, bonds, other securities as well as corporate rights (property right for participation (share) in the charter fund of a legal entity established pursuant to the legislation of Ukraine or legislation of other countries) expressed in convertible currency;
- money claims and the rights to claims related to contractual obligations, which are guaranteed by the first-class banks and have value in convertible currency confirmed in accordance with the legislation (procedures) of the investor's country or international trade practices;
- any intellectual property rights, value of which in convertible currency is confirmed according to the legislation (procedures) of the investor's country or international trade practices as well as confirmed by expert evaluation in Ukraine, including legalised on the territory of Ukraine copyrights, rights to inventions, utility models, industrial models, product and service trademarks, know-how, etc.;
- the rights to carry our business activity including the rights to use or exploit natural resources granted pursuant to laws or under agreements, value of which in convertible currency is confirmed in accordance with the legislation (procedures) of the investor's country or international trade practices; other valuables according to the legislation of Ukraine.

Article 3. Forms of Foreign Investing

Foreign investing may be carried out through:

- share participation in enterprises established jointly with Ukrainian legal entities and natural persons, or acquisition of shares in existing enterprises;
- creation of enterprises wholly belonging to foreign investors, subsidiaries and other separated structural subdivisions of foreign legal entities, or acquisition of entire ownership of existing enterprises;
- acquisition, except when expressly prohibited by the legislation of Ukraine, of real or personal property, including buildings, apartments, premises, equipment, transport vehicles and other objects of ownership through direct acquisition of property or property complexes, or in the form of stocks, bonds and other securities;
- acquisition of the rights to use land or concessions to exploit natural resources on the territory of Ukraine independently or jointly with Ukrainian legal entities and natural persons;
- acquisition of other property rights;
- economic (entrepreneurial) activity, that is based on Production Sharing Agreements; (Paragraph 7 of Article 3 added by Law of Ukraine of June 08, 2000)
- other forms of investing which are not explicitly prohibited by the legislation of Ukraine, in particular, those based on agreements with business subjects of Ukraine without establishment of legal entities.

Article 4. Objects of Foreign Investments

Foreign investments may be made in any objects, investments into which are not prohibited by the laws of Ukraine.

Article 5. Evaluation of Foreign Investments

Foreign investments and investments of Ukrainian partners, including contributions to charter funds of enterprises, shall be evaluated in foreign convertible currency and Ukrainian currency as agreed upon by the parties on the basis of prices of international markets or Ukrainian market.

Investments in foreign currency shall be translated into the currency of Ukraine at the official rate of exchange, set up by the National Bank of Ukraine.

When re-investing profit, income and other earnings received in the currency of Ukraine from making foreign investments, investments shall be translated at the official exchange rate of Ukraine, established by the National Bank of Ukraine at the date of re-investments being actually carried out.

Article 6. Legislation on Investment Activity of Foreign Investors on the Territory of Ukraine

Relations arising out of foreign investments in Ukraine are regulated by this Law, other legislative acts or international agreements of Ukraine. If an international agreement of Ukraine establishes rules other than those stipulated by the Ukrainian legislation for investment activity, provisions of the international agreement shall prevail.

Section II. Government Guarantees to Protect Foreign Investments

Article 7. Legal Regime of Investment Activity

Except for the cases envisaged by Ukrainian laws and international agreements of Ukraine, a national regime for investment and other business activities shall be established on the territory of Ukraine.

A privileged regime of investment and other business activities may be established for individual business entities which implement investment projects with involvement of foreign investments to be realised under the state programs of development of priority branches of economy, social sphere and territories.

Ukrainian laws may determine territories where activities of foreign investors and enterprises with foreign investments are limited or forbidden proceeding from the national security requirements.

Article 8. Guarantees against Changes in Legislation

Should the future special legislation of Ukraine on foreign investments change the guarantees of protection of foreign investments, as prescribed in Section II of this Law, then, if demanded by a foreign investor, the government guarantees to protect foreign investments indicated in this Law shall be applied during ten years period from the date such legislation takes effect.

Rights and liabilities of the parties of the Production Sharing Agreement are regulated by the legislation of Ukraine acting at the moment of signing of the Production Sharing Agreement. The above-mentioned guarantees may not be disseminated to changes in legislation in the area of defence, national security, public order security, and environmental protection.

(Second part of Article 8 added by Law of Ukraine of June 08, 2000)

93

Article 9. *Guarantees against Compulsory Requisitions as well as Unlawful Actions of Government Bodies and their Officials*

Foreign investments in Ukraine are not subject to nationalisation. Government bodies are not entitled to requisition of foreign investments, except for emergency measures in case of a calamity, accident, epidemic, epizootic. The above-mentioned requisition may be enforced on the basis of decisions of bodies authorised to do so by the Cabinet of Ministers of Ukraine.

Decisions on requisition of foreign investments and compensation conditions may be appealed against in court according to Article 26 of this Law.

Article 10. *Compensation and Indemnification of Losses incurred by Foreign Investors*

Foreign investors are entitled to compensation for losses, including lost benefit or moral damage incurred by them due to actions, omissions or improper fulfilment by Ukrainian government bodies or their officials of obligations required by law, with respect to a foreign investor or enterprise with foreign investments according to the legislation of Ukraine.

All expenses and losses incurred by foreign investors as a result of the actions, specified in Article 9, and in the first part of this Article, shall be indemnified on the basis of current market prices and/or substantiated estimates confirmed by an auditor or auditing firm.

Compensation payable to foreign investor should be prompt, adequate and efficient. Compensation to be paid to foreign investor due to the actions, specified in Article 9 of this Law, is calculated at the moment of termination of the right of property.

Compensation to be paid to foreign investor due to the actions, specified in the first part of this Article, is calculated at the time of actual implementation of the decision to compensate for losses. Amount of compensation is to be paid in the currency in which investments have been made, or in any other currency acceptable for the foreign investor in accordance with the effective legislation of Ukraine on foreign currency. From the moment when the right to compensation emerges and until the moment of its payment, interest is calculated on the amount of compensation according to average interest rate, at which London banks issue loans to the first-class banks in the market of European currencies (LIBOR).

Article 11. *Guarantees in Case of Termination of Investment Activity*

In case of termination of investment activity, a foreign investor is entitled to recovery, not later than in six months from the moment of termination of this activity, of its investments in kind or in the invested currency in the amount of the actual contribution (with account of possible decrease in charter fund) without payment of customs duty, as well as revenues earned on these investments in terms of money or goods at the real market value at the moment of termination of investment activity, unless otherwise is established by the legislation or international agreements of Ukraine.

Article 12. Guarantees for Remittance of Profits, Revenues and Other Assets Obtained in Connection with Foreign Investments

After paying taxes, duties and other mandatory payments, foreign investors are guaranteed the right to free and prompt remittance abroad of their profits, revenues and other assets, legally obtained in connection with foreign investments.

Procedure of remittance of profits, revenues and other assets obtained in connection with foreign investments is established by the National Bank of Ukraine.

Section III. State Registration and Control over carrying out Foreign Investments

Article 13. State Registration of Foreign Investments

State registration of foreign investments is executed by the Government of the Autonomous Republic of Crimea, Regional, Kyiv and Sevastopol City State Administrations during three working days from the moment of actual contribution according to the order, established by the Cabinet of Ministers of Ukraine.

Non-registered foreign investments do not entitle to privileges and guarantees provided by this Law.

Article 14. Refusal of State Registration of Foreign Investments

Refusal of state registration of foreign investments is possible only in case of violation of the established order of registration. Refusal motivated by its inexpediency is not allowed.

Refusal of state registration of foreign investments should be documented in written form with indication of reasons for the refusal, and can be appealed against in court.

Article 15. Statistical Reporting on Foreign Investments

Bodies that execute state registration of foreign investments, enterprises with foreign investments, tax and customs authorities and banking institutions submit in compliance with the established forms and deadlines the consolidated statistical reports on foreign investments.

Section IV. Enterprises with Foreign Investments

Article 16. Organisational and Legal Forms of Enterprises with Foreign Investments

Enterprises with foreign investments are established and act on the territory of Ukraine in the forms envisaged by the legislation of Ukraine.

Article 17. Constituent Documents of Enterprises with Foreign Investments

Constituent documents of enterprises with foreign investments shall contain the information envisaged by the legislation of Ukraine for the relevant organisational and legal forms of enterprises as well as the data of nationality of their founders (participants).

Article 18. *Imposition of Duties*

Property imported into Ukraine as contribution of a foreign investor to the charter fund of enterprises with foreign investments (except for the goods for realisation or own consumption) is exempted from duties.

The customs authorities make clearance for entry of such property into the territory of Ukraine based on a promissory note, issued by the enterprise, in the amount of the duty with deferment in payment not more than for 30 calendar days from the date of customs clearance of the import cargo customs declaration.

The promissory note is discharged and import duty is not levied if within the period, assigned for deferment in payment, the above property has been credited to the balance sheet of the enterprise, and the Tax Inspectorate at place of location of the enterprise has made the relevant note on a copy of the promissory note.

Procedure of issuance, recording and discharging of the promissory notes is established by the Cabinet of Ministers of Ukraine.

If within three years from the time of crediting of the foreign investment to the balance sheet of the enterprise with foreign investments, the property, imported in Ukraine as contribution of the foreign investor to the charter fund of the said enterprise, is alienated including in connection with termination of activity of this enterprise (except for exportation of the foreign investment abroad), the enterprise with foreign investments pay import duty calculated on the basis of the customs value of this property, translated into the currency of Ukraine at the official exchange rate of Ukraine established by the National Bank of Ukraine at the date of alienation of the property.

Article 19. *Conditions of Realisation of Products (Works, Services)*

The enterprise with foreign investments determines itself the conditions of realisation of products (works, services) as well as their price unless otherwise is stipulated by the legislation of Ukraine.

Products of enterprises with foreign investments are not subject to licensing and quotation provided they are certified as the products of own manufacturing according to the order, established by the Cabinet of Ministers of Ukraine.

Exportation of the goods subject to the special export regime is carried out in accordance with the legislation of Ukraine.

Article 20. *Taxation*

Enterprises with foreign investments pay the taxes in compliance with the legislation of Ukraine.

Article 21. *Rights of Intellectual Property*

Protection and realisation of intellectual property rights of enterprise with foreign investments are assured pursuant to the legislation of Ukraine. Enterprises with foreign investments make themselves decisions as to patenting (registration) abroad of inventions, industrial models, trademarks and other rights of intellectual property which belong to them according to the legislation of Ukraine.

Section V. Foreign Investments on the Basis of Concessions, Agreements (Contracts) on Production Cooperation, Joint Production and Other Forms of Joint Investment Activity

Article 22. Concession Agreements

The granting of rights to foreign investors to carry out business activity using the objects in the state or communal ownership subject to concession, shall be regulated by applicable legislation of Ukraine and on the basis of a concession agreement.

(Article 22 amended by Law of Ukraine of July 16, 1999)

Article 23. Agreements (Contracts) on Investment Activity

Foreign investors are entitled to enter into agreements (contracts) on joint investment activity (production co-operation, joint production, etc.) which does not involve creation of a legal entity under Ukrainian legislation.

Article 24. Regulation of Business Activity under Agreements (Contracts)

Business activity under agreements (contracts) indicated in Article 23 of this Law shall be regulated by the legislation of Ukraine.

Parties to agreements (contracts) shall keep a separate accounting and reporting on operations related to fulfilment of these agreements (contracts), but they shall open special accounts in banking institutions of Ukraine to make settlements under these agreements (contracts).

Agreements (contracts) shall be registered within the deadlines and in the order established by the Cabinet of Ministers of Ukraine.

Property (except for goods for realisation or own consumption) imported into Ukraine by foreign investors for the period not less than three years with the purpose of investing on the basis of registered agreements (contracts) are exempted from duty in the order envisaged by parts two and three of Article 18 of this Law. In case of alienation of such property earlier than three years from the moment when it was credited to the balance sheet the duty shall be paid in the order envisaged by part five of Article 18 of this Law.

Profits from the joint investment activity under agreements (contracts) shall be subject to taxation in accordance the legislation of Ukraine.

Section VI. Foreign Investments in Special (Free) Economic Zones

Article 25. Regulation of Foreign Investments in Special (Free) Economic Zones

Specific rules for regulations of foreign investments in special (free) economic zones are established by the Ukrainian legislation on special (free) economic zones. Legal regime of foreign investments established in special (free) economic zones shall not create any conditions for investments and carrying out business activity which are less favourable than those stipulated by this Law.

97

Section VII. Settlement of Disputes

Article 26. Procedure of the Settlement of Disputes

Disputes between foreign investors and the state on issues of state regulation of foreign investments and the activities of enterprises with foreign investments shall be subject to consideration in courts of Ukraine unless otherwise specified by the international treaty to which Ukraine is a party.

All other disputes shall be subject to consideration in courts and/or *arbitrazh* courts of Ukraine or, upon agreement of the Parties, in conciliatory courts including foreign courts.

Article 27. Final Provisions

To recognise as invalidated:

- The Law of Ukraine "On Foreign Investments" (Vidomosti Verkhovnoyi Rady Ukrainy, 1992, No. 26, p. 357);
- The Decree of the Cabinet of Ministers of Ukraine "On the Regime of Foreign Investments" of May 20, 1993, No. 55-93 (Vidomosti Verkhovnoyi Rady Ukrainy, 1993, No. 28, p. 302);
- The Law of Ukraine "On the State Program of Encouragement of Foreign Investments in Ukraine" (Vidomosti Verkhovnoyi Rady Ukrainy, 1994, No. 6, p. 28)

Signed
L. Kuchma
President of Ukraine
March 19, 1996 No. 93/96 - BP

Investment Related Treaties of Ukraine

Country	Investment Protection Agreements	Trade Agreements	Free Trade Agreements	Double Taxation Agreements
Algeria	Neg.	01.07.93 22.03.94	Neg.	11.06.88*[61] 05.04.89
Argentina	09.08.95 11.04.97	27.10.95 01.11.96.	Neg.	Neg
Armenia	07.10.94 02.06.95	1996	07.10.94 05.05.96	14.05.96 19.11.96
Australia	Neg.	17.03.98	Neg.	Neg.
Austria	08.11.96 01.12.97	31.08.93	Neg.	16.10.97 20.05.99
Azerbaijan	24.03.97 16.10.97	1996	28.07.95 12.07.96	Neg.
Belarus	 06.12.96	23.12.93 (annexed)	17.12.92 22.12.92	20.12.94
Belgium/Luxembourg	20.05.96 26.02.97	14.06.94 10.11.94	Neg.	20.05.96 25.02.99
Brazil	Neg.	25.10.95 01.11.96	Neg.	Neg.
Bulgaria	08.12.94 20.10.95	20.11.95 01.11.96	Neg.	20.11.95 03.10.97
Canada	24.10.94 02.06.95	31.03.94 20.06.95	Neg.	04.03.96 22.08.96
Chile	30.10.95 15.11.96	03.05.99	Neg.	Neg.
China, People's Republic of	Neg.	15.06.93	Neg.	04.12.95 18.10.96
Chinese Taipei	31.10.92	08.08.92	Neg.	12.07.96
Croatia	15.12.97	02.06.94	Neg.	17.03.99
Cuba	20.05.95 15.11.96	20.08.98	Neg.	Neg.
Cyprus	Neg.	22.02.2000	Neg.	29.10.82* 26.08.83
Czech Republic	17.03.94 20.10.95	17.03.94	Neg.	Neg.

Annex 2
Investment Related Treaties of Ukraine (*cont.*)

Country	Investment Protection Agreements	Trade Agreements	Free Trade Agreements	Double Taxation Agreements
Denmark	23.10.92	14.06.94 10.11.94	Neg.	05.03.96 21.08.96
Egypt	22.12.92	24.12.92	Neg.	Neg.
Estonia	15.02.95 02.06.95	26.05.92 10.12.93	24.05.95 06.02.96	10.05.96 24.12.96
Finland	14.05.92 31.01.94	14.05.92	Neg.	14.10.94 14.12.94
France	02.06.95 26.01.96	14.06.94 10.11.94	Neg.	04.03.70* 01.07.71
Georgia	09.01.95 02.06.95	06.08.92	05.05.96 04.06.96	14.02.97 01.04.99
Germany	15.02.93 29.06.96	14.06.94 10.11.94	Neg.	03.07.95 04.10.96
Greece	01.09.94 04.12.96	15.01.92 15.01.92	Neg.	Neg.
Great Britain	10.02.93 10.02.94	14.06.94 10.11.94	Neg.	10.02.93 11.08.93
Guinea	Neg.	04.11.94 09.02.96	Neg.	Neg.
Hungary	11.10.94 20.12.96	31.05.91	Neg.	19.05.95 24.06.96
India	signed, not ratified	27.03.92 27.03.92	Neg.	Neg.
Indonesia	11.04.96 11.04.97	11.04.96 11.04.97	Neg.	11.04.96 09.11.98
Iran	21.05.96 11.04.97	26.04.92 22.03.94	Neg.	22.05.96 06.12.96
Ireland	Neg.	14.06.94 10.11.94	Neg.	Neg.
Israel	16.06.94 15.11.96	11.07.95 05.05.96	Neg.	Neg.
Italy	02.05.95 12.09.97	14.06.94 10.11.94	Neg.	Neg.
Kazakhstan	17.09.94 09.01.97	21.09.95	17.09.94 04.03.98	09.07.96 14.04.97
Kyrgyzstan	23.02.93	19.06.96 18.09.96	26.05.95 09.12.97	16.10.97 01.05.99
Kuwait	Neg.	Neg.	Neg.	Neg.
Latvia	24.07.97 18.12.97	04.08.92 04.08.92	21.11.95 15.01.97	21.11.95 21.11.96
Lebanon	02.03.2000	25.03.96 26.02.97	Neg.	Neg.

Annex 2

Investment Related Treaties of Ukraine (*cont.*)

Country	Investment Protection Agreements	Trade Agreements	Free Trade Agreements	Double Taxation Agreements
Libya	Neg.	18.01.95 20.10.95	Neg.	Neg.
Lithuania	08.02.94 08.02.95	08.02.94	04.08.93 21.11.95	23.09.96 25.12.97
FYRMacedonia	02.03.98 10.02.2000	03.06.97 16.01.98	Neg.	Neg.
Moldova	29.08.95 20.05.96	09.12.94 27.05.96	29.08.95 27.05.96	29.08.95 27.05.96
Mongolia	05.11.92 05.11.92	19.05.92	Neg.	Neg.
Netherlands	14.07.94 01.05.97	14.06.94 10.11.94	Neg.	24.10.95 02.11.96
Norway	Neg.	26.01.98	Neg.	07.03.96 18.09.96
Poland	12.01.93 14.09.93	04.10.91 04.02.94	Neg.	12.01.93 11.03.94
Portugal	Neg.	14.06.94 10.11.94	Neg.	Neg.
Republic of Korea	16.12.96 16.10.97	30.11.95 11.04.97	Neg.	Neg.
Romania	23.02.95	19.04.94	Neg.	29.03.96 17.11.96
Russian Federation	21.11.98 15.12.99	24.01.95	24.06.93 08.02.95	08.02.95 03.08.99
Slovakia	27.06.94 18.01.96	26.08.93	Neg.	23.01.96 22.11.96
Slovenia	30.03.99 02.03.2000	28.08.96 02.05.97	Neg.	Neg.
South Africa	Neg.	23.11.98	Neg.	Neg.
Spain	26.02.98 10.02.2000	14.06.94 07.10.96	Neg.	Neg.
Sri-Lanka	Neg.	10.08.99	Neg.	Neg.
Sweden	15.08.95 25.12.96	14.06.94 10.11.96	Neg.	14.10.94 14.12.94
Switzerland	20.04.95 21.01.97	20.07.95 01.12.96	Neg.	Neg.
Tadjikistan	Neg.	02.02.95	Neg.	Neg.
Tunus	Neg.	07.12.93	Neg.	Neg.
Turkey	27.11.96 17.05.97	04.05.92 07.03.95	Neg.	27.11.96 29.04.98

Annex 2

Investment Related Treaties of Ukraine (*cont.*)

Country	Investment Protection Agreements	Trade Agreements	Free Trade Agreements	Double Taxation Agreements
Turkmenistan	29.01.98 09.09.99	19.01.95	05.11.94 18.12.96	29.01.98 21.10.99
United Arab Emirates	26.03.96	20.03.95 29.06.97	Neg.	Neg.
United States of America	06.05.92 06.05.92 OPEC; 04.03.94 16.11.96	06.05.92 06.05.92	Neg.	Neg.
Uzbekistan	20.02.93 26.05.94	10.11.94	29.12.94 20.01.96	10.11.94 25.07.95
Vietnam	08.06.94 08.12.94	23.01.92 22.03.94	Neg.	08.04.96 19.11.96
FRYugoslavia	30.10.96	01.08.95 01.11.96	Neg.	Neg.

Key Organisations, Contact Points in Ukraine on Foreign Investment Issues, Some Useful Internet Sites

Ukrainian Government

State Secretary of Cabinet
Victor Lisistsky
Tel: 380-44-2262246
Fax: 380-44-2930211
E-mail: lys@kmu.gov.ua

Ministry of Economy
Serhiy Tihipko
Minister
12/2, hrushevskoho vul.
Kiev 252008, Ukraine
Tel: (380-44) 293-9394, 226-2315
Fax: (380-44) 226-3181
http://www.me.gov.ua

Mr. Volodymyr Ihnashchenko
Director
Directorate for International Development and
European Integration
Ministry of Economy of Ukraine
Tel: 00 380 44 234 19 33
Fax: 00 380 44 234 89 32
Email: jn@kinach.kiev.ua

State Anti-Monopoly Committee
Olexander L Zavada
Chairman
Tel: 380-44-2125054
Fax: 380-44-2124805
E-mail: root@comitet.kiev.ua

State Statistics Committee
Oleksandr Osaulenko
Chairman
3, shota rustaveli vul., Kiev 252023, Ukraine
Tel: (380-44) 227-2433, 226-2021
Fax: (380-44) 227-4266

State Property Fund
Oleksandr Bondar
Chairman
18/9 kutuzova vul.
Kiev 252133, Ukraine
Tel: (380-44) 295-1274, 296-6401
Fax: (380-44) 295-1274
url: www.spfu.com

National Bank of Ukraine
Volodymyr Stelmakh
Chairman
9, instytutska vul., Kiev 252007, Ukraine
Tel: (380-44) 226-2914, 293-5973
Fax: (380-44) 293-1698
url: www.nbu.kiev.ua

OECD

Rainer GEIGER
Deputy Director
Directorate for Financial, Fiscal and Enterprise Affairs
Organisation for Economic Co-operation and Development
2, rue André Pascal
75016 - Paris
Tel: (331) 45.24.91.03
Fax: (331) 45.24.91.51

Mehmet Ögütçü
Principal Administrator
Global Forum on International Investment
OECD, Paris
Tel: 00-33-1-45249395
Fax: 00-33-1-45249335
mehmet.ogutcu@oecd.org

INTERNATIONAL/REGIONAL ORGANISATIONS

European Bank for Reconstruction and Development

Andrew Siton
Country Director for Ukraine
Marykay Fuller, Deputy Head of Office
27/23 sofiivska vul.
Kiev 252001, Ukraine
Tel: (380-44) 464-0132
fax: (380-44) 464-0813
e-mail: kiev@kev.ebrd.com
http://www.ebrd.com

International Finance Corporation

Olena Voloshyna, head of operations
Dmytro Kryshchenko, resident representative, corporate finance services
Amanda Leness, project manager, post-privatisation project
4, bohomoltsa vul., 5th floor
Kiev 252024, Ukraine
Tel: (380-44) 293-4355, 293-0662, 293-0657
fax: (380-44) 247-5630
http://www.ifc.org

International Monetary Fund

Patrick Lenain, senior resident representative
Goohoon Kwon, resident representative
24/7 institutska vul., suites 6 and 8
Kiev 252008, Ukraine
Tel: (380-44) 247-7007
fax: (380-44) 247-7005
http://www.imf.org

Others

Harvard Institute for International Development
10b, khreshchatyk vul., Kiev 252001, Ukraine
Tel: (380-44) 228-8660, 228-1349
fax: (380-44) 228-1349
e-mail: hiid@hiid.kiev.ua
http://www.harvard.kiev.ua

Petro Matiaszek
Chief of Party
Deloitte Touche Tohmatsu
USAID Commercial Law Center Project
(+380.44) 490.6575, fax 490.6574
vul. Shovkovychna, 42-44
Kiev, Ukraine 01004
e-mail: pm@dtt-clc.kiev.ua
www.commerciallaw.com.ua

Toms & Co
18/1 Prorizna Street, Apt. 1
Kiev 01034 Ukraine
Tel: (380-44) 228-1000
(380-44) 490-6000
Fax: (380-44) 228-6508
E-mail: bt@bctoms.com

Alexander Kirilkin
Editor of Interfax-Ukraine Daily & Weekly Business Reports,
Reitarska street 8/5a, UA-01034, Kiev-034, Ukraine
tel: +380+44+4640579(80)
fax:+380+44+4640569
email: decni@interfax.kiev.ua
www.interfax.kiev.ua

Some Useful Internet Sites

Cabinet of Ministers of Ukraine, contains
information on composition of the government,   *http://www.kmu.gov.ua*
Action Plan, legal provisions with short
description of draft documents.

Inter-Agency Council for Economic Reforms
in Ukraine - organisation that provides the
Cabinet of Ministers of Ukraine with   *http://www.reforms.kiev.ua*
consultations and analysis on economic
reforms. Also contains information on
economic transition, draft laws, and more.

Ukrainian legislation, constitution of Ukraine,
VR library, VR press releases, links to foreign   *http://www.Rada.Kiev.UA/welcome.html*
parliaments including EU MS, USA, Belarus,
Russia and international organisations.

Trade Mission of Ukraine in the United States -
country profile, economic reports, market and   *http://www.brama.com/ua-trade-mission/*
legal information, trade and investment
opportunities.

Ministry of Economy	*http://www.me.gov.ua*
Ministry of Health	*http://www.health.gov.ua*
Ministry of Defence	*http://www.dod.niss.gov.ua*
Ministry of Fuel and Energy	*http://www.energy.gov.ua*
Ministry of Labour and Social Policy	*http://www.mlsp.kiev.ua*
Ministry of Emergencies	*http://www.mns.gov.ua*
Ministry of Finance	*http://www.minfin.gov.ua*
Ministry of Science and Technology	*http://www.mstu.gov.ua*
Ministry of Justice	*http://www.minjust.gov.ua*
Ministry Internal Affairs	*http://www.mia.gov.ua/*
Ministry of Foreign Affairs	*http://www.mfa.gov.ua*
The State Property Fund of Ukraine	*http://www.spfukraine.com/* *http://www.ukrmassp.kiev.ua/*
National Bank of Ukraine	*http://www.bank.gov.ua/*
Ukraine Development Gateway (portal site)	*http://www.ukraine-gateway.org.ua*
Basic overview	*http://www.ukraine.org/*

General information about Ukraine

http://www.uazone.net

Online Ukraine/Informational server. Offers newsline, press releases, weather forecast, wide rang of media links (agencies, radio, TV, press)

http://www.online.com.ua/

DZI - the Ukrainian research, information and expert centre in the field of Foreign Trade. Established by the Ministry for Foreign Economic Relations and Trade of Ukraine.

http://www.ukrdzi.com.ua/

European Business Association, linking and representing in Ukraine the major European companies.

http://www.eba.com.ua

Prime portal for Information and Business news by the Kyiv Post publishers

http://www.business.com.ua

Detailed US business review on Ukraine

http://tradeport.org/ts/countries/ukraine/
http://www.infoukes.com/index.shtml

North American Site on Ukraine, contains several links on culture and business.

http://www.uspp.ukrnet.net

Ukrainian League of Entrepreneurs and Industrialists (in Ukrainian)

Harvard Ukraine Project aims at both policy implementation and building the Ukrainian government's capacity to produce analyses and initiate reforms.

http://www.harvard.org.ua

Informational Support for Ukrainian Land Reform http://myland.org.ua/en/ Ukraine Consulting Network, established with the help of the International Finance Corporation.

http://www.consulting.kiev.ua/

DAI is contracted by USAID to manage the NEWBIZNET Project. This program advises and supports a number of regional Business Associations from across Ukraine to grow, strengthen themselves and lobby for improvements in Ukraine's business environment.

http://www.dai.kiev.ua

OECD-Ukraine Forum on Investment and Enterprise Development
Co-chaired by the OECD and the Government of Ukraine

Forum Membership (Indicative)

OECD Secretariat
Donor OECD Member countries
International/regional organisations
Private sector companies and associations (foreign and domestic alike)
Civil Society Groups

Ukraine's Relevant Government Agencies

Supreme Rada
Secretariat of the Cabinet of Ministers
Ministry of Economy
Ministry of Finance
State Customs Administration
State Property Fund
State Anti-Monopoly Committee
Ministry of Justice
State SME Committee

Other members that could wish to contribute.

Terms of Reference

- Monitor the implementation of the Investment Policy Review recommendations and provide further practical advice and assistance to Ukraine
- Identify priority areas for co-operation and provide guidance for specific follow-up projects
- Exchange of experience on best practices for investment promotion
- Review investment trends and policies in Ukraine, taking into account the global situation
- Review obstacles to business development and follow up the implementation
- Create sub-groups as necessary
- Publish an annual progress report on the Forum's activities

Notes

1. The Central Europe Annual 2001, Business Central Europe, January, 2001, p. 54.
2. "President Kuchma expects economic growth to strengthen this year", Ukrainian News, 5 January 2001, Kyiv.
3. Often in order for the authorities to issue such permits and licenses special expertise in a particular sector is required. It is difficult to imagine how one agency can issue permits and licenses for law practice, subsoil exploration and production, alcohol production, etc., as well as conduct fire, sanitary or labour inspections in order to grant respective clearances.
4. *Private Sector Development Journal*, Suppl. No. 1, 1998 (OECD).
5. OECD, Paris, 1999.
6. These recommendations include some of the proposals submitted on 5 February 2001 to the Ukrainian Government by the Privatisation Advisory Group in Kiev consisting of the European Commission, the IMF, the World Bank Group, the GTZ and some bilateral OECD donor countries.
7. The OECD's "Policy Guidelines and Recommendations on Entrepreneurship and Enterprise Development in Transition Economies" (Paris, 1999) could provide some guidance.
8. This represents about 18 per cent of the population of the former Soviet Union. Ukrainians make up about 73 per cent of the total; ethnic Russians number about 20 per cent.
9. Due to the unreliability of pre-transition statistics one could however assume that the 1990 GDP level was probably overestimated, while the 1998 official GDP size was underestimated as a result of the "shadow" economy.
10. "Year-end inflation in Ukraine a high 25.8 per cent, says a senior government official", Associated Press, 31 December 2000, Kyiv.
11. Source: IMF and EBRD.
12. Ukraine conducted a successful renegotiation of its foreign debt in the first quarter of 2000. It had been left facing a peak of repayments during 2000-01 and would certainly have defaulted in the absence of an agreement. The deal was noteworthy in part because of the insistence by official creditors that the private sector bondholders participate in a restructuring. The new agreement will do little to reduce Ukraine's gross foreign debt, which stands a little over 40 per cent of GDP. Following this rescheduling Ukraine expects to resume borrowing from the IMF and other financial institutions including the World Bank and EBRD.
13. "Supporting Reform in Ukraine", James D. Wolfensohn, 25 October 2000.

14. Agribusiness and food processing and packaging sectors have potential to become areas of significant growth. However, this potential growth is very much dependent on the government's commitment to a real privatisation policy in agriculture and rapid implementation of that policy. Agricultural reform has stalled in recent years, and many producers remain heavily indebted to the government for past deliveries of agricultural inputs.

15. The energy sector potentially can also attract a high level of investment. Opportunities in the electrical power area can be significant if and when restructuring and privatisation take hold. The passage of Production Sharing Agreement (PSA) legislation in July 1999 has improved prospects for significant foreign investment in oil, gas and coal production.

16. A mini-construction boom of "dachas" and apartment renovations, characteristic of an emerging economy, will create demand for quality building products, hand-held construction equipment, finishing materials, etc.

17. Telecommunications, computers, and computer software are other important growth sectors. As Ukraine attempts to merge onto the international information "superhighway," Ukrainian enterprises will require complete solutions to their information processing needs.

18. See EBRD, 1999 Transition Report, Table 6.1. at p. 116.

19. See EBRD, *ibid*, chart 6.1. at p. 117.

20. See Siedenberg, Hoffmann (eds.), "Ukraine at the Crossroad", New York 1999, p. 146 ff.

21. See Vennen "Report on Impediments to Foreign Investment in Ukraine", Kiev, August 1999, p.3.

22. This survey was performed by the Flemings/SARS Consortium within the technical assistance component of the Enterprise Development Adjustment Loan from the World Bank in December 1999-January 2000. Respondents included 34 large foreign direct investors who had entered or were seeking to enter Ukraine's market.

23. See Annex 1 for a list.

24. A full description of these measures, with completed references to the corresponding law or other state provision, is contained in the "Blue Book" of Non-Conforming Measures Maintained by Contracting Parties to the ECT, which can be viewed on the Energy Charter web-site: *http://www.encharter.org*

25. The EC argued that the import restrictions violated the Partnership and Co-operation Agreement between Ukraine and the EC.

26. The largest areas are: Sivash and "The Port of Crimea" on Crimea, "Donetsk" and "Asov" in Donetsk Region, "Zakarpattia" in Zakarptsky region, "Yavoriv" and "Kurortopolis Truskavets" in Lviv Region, "Slavutich" in Kiev Region, "Interport Kovil" in Volyn Region, "Mikolaiv" in Mikolaiv city and "Porto-Franko" in Odessa city.

27. See ICPS Policy Studies, July-August 1999, p. 27 ff for further details.

28. "Openness to foreign investment in Ukraine", see at *www.bisnis.doc.gov/bisnis/country/ukchapterViii.htm*

29. Private law is understood as the body of law that addresses legal relationships between or among private individuals and enterprises; it is distinguished from public law which governs state authorities, including the latters' relationships with private individuals and enterprises.

30. For further details see Frishberg Guide, p. 40 ff.

31. For example, Ukrainian legislation limits foreign participation to 49 per cent or less in certain sectors such as publishing houses, insurance and privatised public "strategic" enterprises.

32. See IFC Survey, p. 9 ff.

33. For further details, see Vennen Report, p. 9 ff.

34. Law "On the Protection of Rights to Inventions and Useful Models", Law "On the Protection of Rights to Industrial Designs", and Law "On the Protection of Rights to Trade and Service Marks".

35. See for further details, USAID Report, p. 14 ff.

36. See Siedenberg-Hoffman, *ibid*.

37. Seven of the Council's 14 members are appointed by the President, and the other 7 are elected by Parliament for seven-year terms. The Chairman is elected by the Council. Decisions are taken by a simple majority.

38. Kyiv Post, 6 July 2000, p 3B.

39. For details, see Frishberg Guide, p. 224 ff.

40. For further details, see Frishberg memorandum on the Law "On Foreign Economic Activities and Import/Export contracts".

41. For more specifics, see Vennen Report, p. 12 ff.

42. For a detailed overview of the PCA, see UEPLAC, "Guide to the Implementation of the Partnership and Co-operation Agreement between Ukraine and the European Community", Kiev 1999.

43. The BSEC was created in June 1992 as an informal regional co-operation network and reconstituted in June 1998 as a full-fledged international organisation.

44. These are: Austria, Argentina, Armenia, Bulgaria, Canada, Estonia, Finland, Krygyzstan, Latvia, Moldova, Russia and Switzerland.

45. For further details, see Frishberg Memorandum on "Ukrainian Currency Regulations".

46. Privatisation certificates were issued free of charge to all Ukrainian citizens; and compensation certificates were issued in 1994 to the holders of Ukrainian currency bank deposits in order to compensate them for the losses due to the hyperinflationary devaluation of the karbovanets.

47. See USAID Report, p. 9 ff.

48. See EBRD, Transition Report 1999, p. 115 ff.

49. See EBRD, Transition Report 1999, chart 6.3. at p. 119.

50. *Ibid*, chart 6.8. at p. 120.

51. *Ibid*, table 6.2. at p. 123.

52. *Ibid*, chart 6.9. at p. 124.

53. *Ibid*, table 6.3. at p. 125.

54. For a more comprehensive account on and recommendations for institutional reforms, see German Advisory Group, p. 140 ff.

55. For specifics, see Vennen Report, pp. 4, 5.

56. For further specifics, see IFC Survey, p. 10 ff.

57. See IFC Survey, p. 50 ff.
58. See for details, USAID Report, p. 22 ff.
59. See Siedenberg – Hoffman, p. 109 ff for specifics.
60. See World Bank Country Study, p. 23 ff with further details.
61. Treaties concluded by USSR and succeeded by Ukraine.

OECD PUBLICATIONS, 2, rue André-Pascal, 75775 PARIS CEDEX 16
PRINTED IN FRANCE
(14 2001 10 1 P) ISBN 92-64-18673-5 – No. 51813 2001